MW00998512

EERO SAARINEN

An Architecture of Multiplicity

Antonio Román

Princeton Architectural Press | New York

Published by
Princeton Architectural Press
37 East Seventh Street
New York, New York 10003

For a free catalog of books, call 1.800.722.6657.
Visit our web site at www.papress.com.

This book was published with the assistance of the Graham Foundation
for Advanced Studies in the Fine Arts.

Project coordinator: Mark Lamster
Project editor: Alanna Stang
Research: Linda Lee & Megan Carey
Proofreader: Noel Millea
Design: David Konopka

Special thanks to:
Nettie Aljian, Ann Alter, Nicola Bednarek, Janet Behning, Penny Chu,
Russell Fernandez, Clare Jacobson, Nancy Eklund Later, Jane Sheinman,
Katharine Smalley, Scott Tennant, Jennifer Thompson, Joe Weston, and
Deb Wood of Princeton Architectural Press
—Kevin C. Lippert, publisher

Library of Congress Cataloging-in-Publication Data
Román, Antonio.
    Eero Saarinen : an architecture of multiplicity / Antonio Román.— 1st
ed.
        p. cm.
    Includes bibliographical references and index.
    ISBN 1-56898-340-9 (alk. paper)
    1. Saarinen, Eero, 1910-1961—Criticism and interpretation. 2.
Architecture—United States—20th century. 3. Eclecticism in
architecture. I. Title.
    NA737.S28 R66 2003
    720'.92—dc21
                        2002014785

Image Credits

ii. John Zimmerman/TimePix; vi. courtesy of Knoll; viii. Joseph Molitor, Columbia University; 4. Glen Paulsen; 6. Ken Hedrich, Hedrich-Blessing collection of the Chicago Historical Society; 11. Saarinen Archive; 16. Charles R. Shulze; 17. Saarinen Archive; 22, 24–27. Deere & Company; 32–35, 38–39. IBM Corporate Archives; 40. Joseph Molitor, Columbia University; 46–47. Saarinen Archive; 48 (bottom left). courtesy of Cranbrook Archive; 50. courtesy of Lambert-St. Louis International Airport; 54–59. Saarinen Archive; 68. courtesy of Knoll; 74–75. Julius Shulman; 76. top: The Mies van der Rohe Archive, the Museum of Modern Art, New York. Gift of the architect. © 2002 the Museum of Modern Art, New York. middle: Richard Shirk, courtesy of Cranbrook Archives. bottom: Arts & Architecture, Columbia University; 78. Saarinen Archive; 82. Joseph Molitor, Columbia University; 84, 86–87. Saarinen Archive; 94–95. The Museum of Modern Art, New York. Gift of the designers. © 2002 the Museum of Modern Art, New York; 96–98, 100–104. courtesy of Knoll; 106. Deere & Company; 112. Joseph Molitor, Columbia University; 114. Saarinen Archive; 115. DaimlerChrysler Historical Collection; 124, 126–132, 134–139. Jefferson National Expansion Memorial/National Park Service; 140. Ministero per i Beni e le Attivita Culturali; 141. Jefferson National Expansion Memorial/National Park Service; 142, 146 (top). Cowles Library, Drake University; 146 (middle and bottom). Hedrich-Blessing collection of the Chicago Historical Society; 147. Saarinen Archive; 148. Ben Schnall, Special Collections, Vassar College Libraries; 149. Cowles Library, Drake University; 150. Brandeis University; 152–154. Alexander Georges, Concordia College; 155. Ben Schnall, Special Collections, Vassar College Libraries; 156. Glen Paulsen; 158. Columbia University; 159–161. Glen Paulsen; 162. Saarinen Archive; 166, 168. © 2001 General Motors Corporation. Used with permission of GM Media Archives; 172. CBS Photo Archive; 174–175, 178–179. Saarinen Archive; 181. CBS Photo Archive; 182. Stephens College Archive; 186, 188. © Australian Tourist Commission; 192. © Raimondo Borea; 202. Ken Hedrich, Hedrich-Blessing collection of the Chicago Historical Society; 206–208. Courtesy of Milwaukee War Memorial Center; 210. North Christian Church; 211. Alexander Georges, Concordia College.

Captions to chapter opening images

Creating: Chapel, MIT, Cambridge, MA, 1950–55. Screen by Harry Bertoia Ezra Stoller © Esto

Dwelling: Executive Chair, Knoll Associates, 1957

Building: John Deere & Company Headquarters, Moline, IL, 1957–63 Construction

Socializing: Hubbell Dining Hall, Drake University, Des Moines, IA, 1947–50

Judging: Chapel, Stephens College, Columbia, MO, 1953–57

TO MY PARENTS

CONTENTS

FOREWORD
IGNASI DE SOLÀ-MORALES*

The purpose of Antonio Román's research has been to explore the architectural mechanisms by means of which an architect can produce a valuable body of work, despite Its apparent lack of unity. This question is especially relevant today, when pluralism constitutes a respected value and where a multiplicity of languages inevitably coexist, not only in the same place or in the trajectory of a certain architect, but even in the same piece of work.

The critical and historiographic recognition of Eero Saarinen and much of his oeuvre is beyond doubt, but on more than one occasion his work had been labeled eclectic or "styleless." Moreover, Saarinen's work, though well-known and documented, has previously lacked a profound academic treatment that would define it as a whole. Tackling the issue of pluralism in modern architecture is a virtually limitless and impossible task. Employing Saarinen's work as a case study, on the other hand, was a thoroughly justifiable exercise in reflection.

Each of the chapters highlights one or more of Saarinen's works in order to study them in minute detail from a particular viewpoint. Thus, notions such as diversity, style, subjectivity, creativity, dwelling, building, socializing, and judgment become meaningful at the same time that they become theoretical tools capable of penetrating into the profound significance, beyond stylistic appearance, of Saarinen's body of work.

The quality of the finished product, after long years dedicated to the task, is, I believe, beyond any doubt.

*Ignasi de Solà-Morales, professor of architectural theory at the Universitat Politècnica de Catalunya, whose death in 2001 was a great loss to so many, was my principal advisor during the research for this project. His academic report is excerpted here with his family's permission.

This book was born of a genuine affinity for Eero Saarinen and his work. In an architectural climate that still betrays the influence of neorationalism and postmodernism, Eero Saarinen's work holds a special fascination for me. If nothing else, this study has revealed him as a key to understanding second-generation architectural modernism and the many issues facing contemporary professional practice.

The examination of Saarinen's life and work was an exceptionally attractive challenge. Though he was one of the leading modernists of the 1950s, achieving a level of recognition beyond that of most of his peers, his work, which invariably defies classification, has received little scholarly attention. Saarinen's sparse commentary on his own work contributed to his image as an enigmatic architect. But despite his reticence, Saarinen's work brought him considerable acclaim—albeit often accompanied by controversy. There are those who consider him a peripheral architect and, unforgivably in their eyes, one of questionable taste. Orthodox modernists certainly never accepted him. For others, however, his fresh approach and willingness to experiment with architectural vocabulary amounted to a new vision of the modern idea that offered up exciting alternatives to the strictures of mainstream postwar architecture.

Educated at Yale University in the Beaux-Arts tradition, Saarinen matured under the influence of his father, Eliel Saarinen. The elder Saarinen, a revered Finnish architect who emigrated to Michigan in 1923, was a driving force behind the experimental Cranbrook Academy in Bloomfield Hills, where the younger Saarinen was raised. As a consequence, perhaps, of these varied influences—a traditional education, his father's modern heterodoxy, a progressive home environment—Saarinen developed a unique approach to his own architectural practice. As he began to design independently—for years Eero had apprenticed with his father—Saarinen took on the mission of broadening the modern vocabulary, of working, in a critical way, to expand an inheritance that, to a great extent, was rooted in functionalism.

Saarinen's career was cut short by his untimely death in 1961 following brain-tumor surgery in Detroit. He was only fifty-one years old. But during his eleven-year independent career, Saarinen undertook near thirty projects in the United States and Europe. He was consistently at the forefront of American building developments and professed a belief in technical progress. Yet his Nordic origins, his education, and an early study trip through Europe endowed him with a historical awareness that informed all of his projects. His eclecticism and his ability to combine pragmatic and existential concerns resonate strongly with the concerns of the postmodern condition in which we are still immersed. Today, the figure of Eero Saarinen is an inescapable referent.

My passion for Saarinen's architecture developed during a period of study at Harvard University, when I had the opportunity to visit a significant number of his buildings in the United States. From MIT's Kresge Chapel in Cambridge to the Dulles International Airport Terminal outside Washington, DC, I was captivated by the stylistic variety of his structures. Unusually moving, Saarinen's architecture eschews a recurrent formal repertoire; diversity is its defining characteristic. Works such as the TWA Terminal at John F. Kennedy Airport, Ezra Stiles and Morse colleges at Yale University, and the CBS Building in New York City seem to have little formal relation. For Saarinen, the development of a consistent signature style was never a priority, though formal consistency was then and remains today one of the primary conventions by which architects are evaluated (indeed, for many architects the development of a "style" is a prime objective). Saarinen was unconcerned with such formal unity. For him, each design was a statement unto itself, a particular, specific solution resolved by particular, specific means. Rather than a mere penchant for stylistic experimentation, the diversity of his work reflects an eclecticism of procedure, an ability to adapt his method of design to a new project and a new program. The TWA Terminal expresses the excitement of jet travel; the Yale colleges reflect the monastic character of university life; the CBS Building exalts the company's presence within the context of Manhattan's unrelenting grid and the skyscraper form.

The diversity of Saarinen's work implies a questioning of the very idea of style, and this is the point of departure for this text. As opposed to a purely formalist examination of his works, my mode of inquiry gives equal weight to the architect's method of design and his creative process. It involves a twofold process of contemplating significant examples of Saarinen's work, in order to discover in them aspects that might have motivated his architectural decisions, and then analyzing the projects in light of those motives. Saarinen's inspiration and the forces that shaped his architectural raison d'être, are, therefore, essential elements of this study.

This methodology crystallized during my fieldwork in the archives at Yale, Cranbrook, and Roche and Dinkeloo, where, most notably, I had the opportunity to examine, respectively: the Eero Saarinen Papers, which include the documents that Aline Saarinen, his widow, employed when editing the architect's posthumous monograph in 1962; the Saarinen Family Papers, assembled by Loja Saarinen, Eero Saarinen's mother; and the Eero Saarinen Archive, which house his firm's project records. Interviews with Saarinen collaborators Cesar Pelli and, above all, Kevin Roche ultimately helped determine the architect's priorities for each project.

Five subjective categories—creating, dwelling, building, socializing, and judging—provide five different perspectives, each of which comprises one chapter, from which Saarinen's individual works can be examined. The first, "creating," is significant in the case of what is probably Saarinen's best-known work: the TWA Terminal (1956–62). In this building, Saarinen devoted particular attention to architectural expression. Here, the architect who described himself as "methodical but not cautious" conveyed the romance of jet travel while pursuing mass and movement effects similar to those explored by architects of the baroque era.

"Dwelling" is a crucial concept in the examination of Stiles and Morse colleges at Yale (1957–62). As Saarinen envisaged it, college-based university life shared many characteristics with monastic life. Removed from functionalist necessity, residence, in the specific context of higher education, acquired an existential dimension. In his furniture, in particular the Womb Chair and Pedestal series (1946–48 and 1955–57, respectively), Saarinen expresses his view on the relationship between comfort and dwelling.

"Building" considers Saarinen's architecture through an examination of technique. As an indefatigable innovator, Saarinen kept himself abreast of all the latest developments in construction technology. The Dulles International Airport, in Chantilly, Virginia (1958–62)—which Saarinen believed to be his most significant work—takes a groundbreaking concrete and suspension-cable structure into the realm of symbolism. And the Jefferson National Expansion Memorial, in Saint Louis, Missouri (1947–65), a parabolic form of stressed skin, assumes a truly monumental dimension as the "Gateway to the West." With Saarinen it is impossible to separate technical and artistic aspects. His work fused the two in a way that validates the notion of *techne*—the conflation of building art and science.

Saarinen's prioritization of the social context was another essential element of his practice. "Socializing" concentrates on two case studies that demonstrate how he adapted his architectural approach to respond to different urban conditions. His first and largest project, the General Motors Technical Center, in Warren, Michigan (1947–56), proposed community life in a suburban milieu. The center's research and development activity, a reflection of American society at the time, advanced the tenets of industrial society. With its uniform vocabulary and superblock conception, this unique complex elaborates on the sleek machine-age architecture of Albert Kahn and Mies van der Rohe. At the end of his career, Saarinen's CBS Building (1960–65) appears as a kind of counterpoint. Set in Manhattan's dense landscape, which had just begun to confront a new formulation of zoning laws, the CBS tower, with its versatile granite facade, becomes a statement that blends effortlessly into its urban context.

Among his many other pronounced traits, Saarinen was a keen and articulate judge of his own work and that of his peers. Through the perspective of "judging," it becomes evident that his powers of persuasion had a decisive influence on the historic Sydney

Opera House competition jury. According to records of the competition proceedings, it is possible to conclude that the jurors chose Danish architect Jørn Utzon largely because of Saarinen's opinionated arguments. Saarinen was similarly judgmental of his own work. Documents related to the American Embassy building in London (1955–60) show how ruthlessly Saarinen judged his own designs, and that he perceived reevaluation to be an essential part of his professional practice. The critical dimension of his personality reveals Saarinen's dialectical relationship with his craft.

In focusing on the unique nature of Saarinen's creative process and the diverse architecture that it engendered, I do not mean to ignore the significance of those who, led by Michel Foucault, have spoken of the so-called death of the author, of the irrelevance of placing the individual subject at the center of study. On the contrary, in the face of the opposition between subjective (generative) and nonsubjective (structural) approaches, I favored a conjunction of both. Thus, for example, in the section on "creating," analysis of the TWA Terminal focuses largely on the generative terrain, specifically Saarinen's ideas and inspiration. However, the project is further assessed in terms of its cultural significance. Each type of analysis pertains then to both perspectives.

Saarinen's multiplicity—his capacity to respond to each new project in an individually appropriate way—is the crux of this study. It involves an assessment of the historiography of his architecture, as well as an exploration of one of the central problems facing architects today: the unity of their work. In each of his projects Saarinen addressed architectural challenges in an apparently eclectic way that can nonetheless be considered unitary—not stylistically or structurally unitary, but unitary according to his personal quest and the unique needs of the project. Within the context of the current value placed on pluralism, Saarinen's multiplicity takes on a special significance. While he never attempted to achieve formal consistency, and he pursued many divergent goals, it is possible to detect in his work a certain unity of purpose—to perceive it as an architecture of multiplicity.

INTRODUCTION

In architecture you have to have great sensibility
and the hide of a rhinoceros.

In the postwar period, when Eero Saarinen began practicing on his own, the modern movement—transformed into an aesthetic and dubbed the "International Style"—was the dominant force in mainstream American architecture. The modernist vision of European masters such as Le Corbusier, Mies van der Rohe, and Walter Gropius developed into a set of formal principles employed as rules of composition. An intellectual process of abstraction based on rationalization, industrialization, and social factors had become simply an architecture of steel and glass, blank surfaces, and all-pervading regularity. Every good architect was expected to hew to this formal line. Thus, as Saarinen started turning out buildings that stylistically and structurally veered off the grid, he quickly became a controversial figure.

Many of Saarinen's contemporaries reproached him for lacking a style of his own, for making "an architecture of many shapes but too few ideas." He was accused of bad taste. The absence of a recurrent formal repertoire amounted to so much incoherence. Reviews could be extremely virulent. One of the most influential scholars, Vincent Scully, criticized buildings such as the Yale Hockey Rink and the Kennedy and Dulles airport terminals for exhibitionism, structural pretension, and self-defeating urbanistic arrogance, and derisively suggested that Saarinen was attempting to reinvent the wheel in each project.[1] Even Frank Lloyd Wright, whose own body of work exhibited considerable diversity, couldn't muster support for Saarinen's eclectic trajectory. Writing to Saarinen's second wife, Aline Saarinen, in 1958, Wright told her to "tell your young architect that I hope he will do something someday that I like."[2]

For other architectural observers, however, Saarinen's architecture evoked admiration. While today we tend to see the postwar period as being dominated by mainstream modernism, many second-generation modernists, including Saarinen, were in fact interested in advancing architecture beyond the homogeneity born of high modernism's tenets. They were attuned to the country's rapidly changing conditions, to the fact that they were living in a time of technical progress when new needs and different interests demanded original design. There were also critics who applauded Saarinen's willingness to experiment formally and stylistically. Henry-Russell Hitchcock, the historian who helped launch the International Style, identified Saarinen, positively, as a modern mannerist.[3] J. M. Richards, another influential historian, heralded him as one of the prominent members of the next generation of modernist architects—a group that included Charles Eames, Louis Kahn, Bruce Goff, Hugh Stubbins, Minoru Yamasaki, Ralph Rapson, John Johansen, I. M. Pei, Paul Rudolph, and Gordon Bunshaft.[4] Peter Blake, an architectural critic of proven independence, viewed Saarinen as "one of the most creative architects of the generation that followed Mies and Corbu."[5] And just after

Saarinen's premature death in 1961, Philip Johnson, the architect and former historian who, with Hitchcock, promoted the International Style, told his widow Aline: "Eero's place is secure. His work will live on its own greatness."[6] In 1962, Saarinen was publicly acclaimed by his peers and posthumously awarded the Gold Medal of the American Institute of Architects, its highest honor.

In spite of, or perhaps because of this controversy, Saarinen's office in Bloomfield Hills, Michigan, became a magnet for aspiring young architects and a spawning ground for future architectural innovators, including Kevin Roche, Cesar Pelli, Robert Venturi, Anthony Lumsden, and Gunnar Birkerts.[7] While the 1950s spirit dictated that a coherent vocabulary was a necessary condition for architectural distinction, some of Saarinen's associates, such as Venturi, regarded him as something of a prophetic figure for the way his buildings evolved from an expanding, project-based vocabulary rather than from some modern functionalist ideal.[8]

If Saarinen was controversial, he was also enigmatic. His professional statements and writings are scarce. Lecture transcripts provide some insight into his architectural conscience, but the bulk of information about his personality derives from his personal writings and the testimony of his collaborators. Of the things that can be said of him with certainty, the first is that his commitment to work and to architecture were absolute: "One has to work as hard as one can," he told a friend in 1952.[9] And indeed he did. The office seemed to be continually on deadline, always *en charrette*, as critic Peter Carter commented.[10] Saarinen's commitment to architecture was a personal obsession. According to Kevin Roche, who worked with Saarinen for eleven years and was one of his main collaborators, Saarinen never stopped demonstrating his passion for architecture: "He was totally absorbed, his conversation was always architecture."[11]

Saarinen was conscious of his singular commitment and often criticized himself for it. He longed to be more versatile, and tried to adapt himself to different situations. For example, "to a group of businessmen, he wouldn't be very artistic, he tried to be another businessman," Roche says.[12] For Saarinen, the ideal architect was a Renaissance humanist. He was nevertheless sanguine about the possibility of mastering the other fields that interested him, such as history, philosophy, or literature, and reconciled himself to the notion that "a person who contributes to culture is not necessarily a cultured person."[13]

Controversial yet enigmatic, instinctive yet methodical, fluent in cutting-edge technology yet steeped in tradition, respectful of his modern heritage yet unencumbered by the force of its cultural dominance: these fascinating dichotomies, which reveal

ABOVE Glen Paulsen. Drawing of Eero Saarinen office, Bloomfield Hills, MI

Saarinen's character and, by extension, his practice, have their antecedents in the contrasting influences of his youth and education. Specifically, his Finnish heritage and his American upbringing, his exposure to Cranbrook's communal ideology and his classical Beaux-Arts training at Yale, and his father's heterodox modernist tendencies. These countervailing influences help explain why Saarinen emerged as an architect with an original approach and a diverse product.

Eero Saarinen was born in 1910 in Kirkkonummi, Finland, to Eliel Saarinen, a prominent Finnish architect and urban planner, himself the son of a Lutheran pastor, and Loja Gesellius, a textile artist trained as a sculptor. Eero's early life was spent in the creative atmosphere of Villa Hvitträsk, the family home his father designed on a wooded bluff overlooking a lake outside Helsinki, which became a center of Finnish artistic life. Eliel Saarinen was critical of the indiscriminate use of different styles so prevalent in nineteenth-century architecture. Instead, his practice drew on the Finnish crafts movement and on modernist currents, particularly those originating in Germany, as his Helsinki Central Station and decentralization plan for Helsinki (1905–14 and 1917–18, respectively) demonstrate. After winning worldwide acclaim with his second prize in the international competition for the Chicago Tribune Tower in 1922, Eliel emerged as a major force in the international architectural community. A year later, he uprooted his professional practice and his young family and emigrated to the United States, initially to Evanston, Illinois, and then to Ann Arbor, Michigan, where he soon developed the buildings and the architectural curriculum of the Cranbrook Academy of Art, an arts school located just outside of the burgeoning city of Detroit. Thus, Eero Saarinen arrived in the United States for the first time in 1923 at the age of twelve.

The Cranbrook Academy of Art was the brainchild of Detroit newspaper publisher George G. Booth and his wife, Ellen. Proponents of the English Arts and Crafts movement and founders, in 1906, of the Detroit Society of Arts and Crafts, the Booths established Cranbrook as a full-fledged school of art and a meeting place for artisans and craftsmen. Gradually the need for development became apparent and the school brought together the teaching of architecture, planning, landscape, drawing, painting, sculpture, ceramics, metalwork, and weaving. It was one of very few institutions in the world at that time to offer a curriculum in which every field of craft and design was represented. With his father as director of the graduate department of architecture and city planning and his mother in charge of the weaving studio, the young Eero Saarinen was immersed in a community devoted to the arts. And, as he matured, there was little doubt that he would follow in his parents' footsteps and choose an artistic path.

At the age of eighteen, when the time came for him to decide on a field of study, Saarinen hesitated briefly over whether to pursue sculpture or architecture before deciding on the former, which he studied in Paris at the Académie de la Grande Chaumière from 1929–30. This Montparnasse atelier was where, inspired by the teaching of Antoine Bourdelle, well-known sculptors like Alberto Giacometti and Alexander Calder also studied. But by the fall of 1931 Saarinen had already changed his mind and enrolled in architecture at Yale University's School of Fine Arts. He completed the four-year curriculum in three years, graduating with honors in 1934.

Unlike the experimental atmosphere at Cranbrook, Yale's architecture program was traditional. The modernist-inspired Bauhaus-type alternative, more radical in breaking with history, came later, when Walter Gropius and Mies van der Rohe emigrated to America, the former taking up a professorship at Harvard in 1937, the latter establishing himself as director of architecture at the Armour Institute in Chicago in 1938. Thus, like nearly all other architecture schools at the time, Yale followed the model of the École des Beaux Arts in Paris, emphasizing design practice above all. Students were regularly required to complete *esquisses* or fast designs, as well as projects, or elaborated designs. And in addition to standard subjects such as theory, history of architecture, archaeological research, calculus, structure, and construction, course requirements included drawing, watercolor, and modeling.[14] At Yale, Saarinen regularly attended lectures by both faculty and visiting scholars; invited speakers included such prestigious historians as Josep Pijoan, Henry Focillon, and Erwin Panofsky.[15] He published several of his academic projects in the Yale Bulletin and entered and won prizes in many of the Beaux-Arts competitions typically held at architecture schools.[16]

Upon completion of his formal studies, Saarinen won the Charles O. Matcham fellowship for European travel. The prize allowed him to travel for two years through parts of the Mediterranean and northern Europe. His visits to Italy, Greece, Egypt, Palestine, Germany, Sweden, and Finland exposed him to the sources of classicism, and his sketches and watercolors reflect his impressions of much of the architecture encountered in these locations. During his stay in Finland he worked for a short period of time with modernist architect Jarl Eklund. In the summer of 1936 Saarinen returned to Cranbrook where his father had by now developed many designs for the buildings on the ever-expanding campus.

Cranbrook was one of the main alternatives to artistic education in the United States, with its wide-ranging course offerings, emphasis on craftsmanship, and communal living arrangement modeled on experimental artists' communities in Europe.[17] Students and teachers, living on campus, shared classes, meals, and activities along

LEFT Saarinen Saarinen with Perkins, Wheeler, and Will. Crow Island School, Winnetka, IL, 1938–40

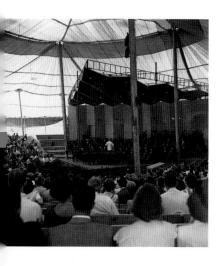

with visiting artists and teachers. Cranbrook had firmly established its reputation as an alternative type of artistic education and a bastion of creative interchange. As a result, innovative artists flocked to its serene campus. Around the time the younger Saarinen was on the faculty, from 1939 to 1940, Cranbrook played host to such sculptors, designers, and architects as Carl Milles, Harry Bertoia, Florence Knoll, Charles and Ray Eames, and Ralph Rapson.

In 1937, after a brief collaboration with New York designer Norman Bel Geddes, Saarinen went to work for his father. Although the apprenticeship was supposed to be largely collaborative, Eero commented that his father did not allow him to design even a staircase on his own until he was thirty-five years old. And it was not until the elder Saarinen's death in 1950, in fact, that the younger would strike out on his own. Nevertheless, the Saarinens, together with J. Robert Swanson (husband of Eero's older sister Pipsan), were named as the winners of the 1939 competition for the extension of the National Gallery in Washington, DC. They also shared credit for the Crow Island School, in Winnetka, Illinois (1939–40).[18] Eero taught architecture for two years at Cranbrook Academy, and then he served at the presentation division of the Office of Strategic Services, in Washington, DC. In 1941 the father-son team formed a partnership, with Swanson, as Saarinen Swanson Saarinen, which lasted seven years. Their designs for colleges and universities included the development plan and a women's dormitory for Antioch College, Yellow Springs, Ohio, in 1945. When Robert and Pipsan Swanson formed a partnership—she was an interior designer—in 1947, the firm's name was reduced to simply Saarinen Saarinen.

In Finland, Eliel Saarinen had been an active participant in the debate about the idea of a national architecture. He defended the so-called National Romantic movement, which paralleled the earlier architecture of H. H. Richardson in the United States. Villa Hvitträsk was clearly inspired by Finnish vernacular architecture. As one of the driving forces in the Cranbrook community, the elder Saarinen embodied an alternative to the more dogmatic modernism emanating from Central Europe. Such a powerful father figure could not help but have a profound impact on his son, and this was the case with the relationship between Eliel and Eero. Indeed, Eero was well aware of his father's influence, at one point telling the *New York Times*, "Except for a rather brief excursion into sculpture it never occurred to me to do anything but to follow in my father's footsteps and become an architect. . . . Until his death in 1950 when I started to create my own form, I worked within the form of my father."[19]

After Eliel's death, Eero Saarinen finally started to work alone. Thanks in part to his father's legacy, the younger Saarinen already had an established name and thriving

ABOVE AND RIGHT Aspen Music Tent, Aspen, Colorado, 1952. © Photo Berko

ABOVE Kresge Auditorium and Chapel, Massachusetts Institute of Technology, Cambridge, MA, 1950–55
Ezra Stoller © Esto
RIGHT Kresge Auditorium. Section

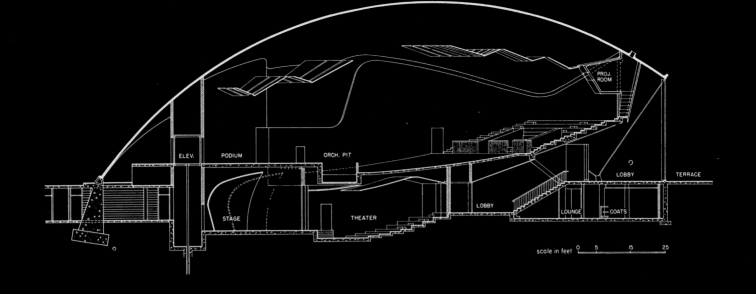

ELEV. PODIUM   ORCH. PIT   PROJ.
                                                                 ROOM

                                                                 LOBBY   TERRACE

                                                          LOBBY

STAGE   THEATER   LOUNGE   COATS

                                        scale in feet 0 5   15   25

practice. Although he had previously entered some competitions independently, such as that for the Jefferson National Expansion Memorial in St. Louis, Missouri, he began working on his first solo commissions in the early 1950s. He quickly made his mark on the profession. By 1956, when the office reached its peak of productivity, there were eighteen projects in various stages of development, including: the General Motors Technical Center, Detroit, MI; Kresge Auditorium and Chapel at MIT, Cambridge, MA; the Milwaukee County War Memorial, Milwaukee, WI; the Noyes Dormitory at Vassar College, Poughkeepsie, NY; the Unites States Chancellery in London, England; the Ingalls Hockey Rink at Yale University, New Haven, CT; and the TWA Terminal at Idlewild (now JFK) Airport. Saarinen's designs for these buildings demonstrate a striking range of formal approaches. As Philip Johnson later said, nobody would believe that many of Saarinen's buildings could be by the same architect "because they represent such violently different attitudes."[20]

For Saarinen, this kind of judgment was not particularly troubling. His approach to style reflected the sentiments of architects such as Frank Lloyd Wright and Le Corbusier, who opposed the notion that style was in itself something to strive for—a philosophy at odds with the formalist historiographical currents of the time, which posited style as consistent formal output.[21] Wright clearly opposed the association of form with style. In his 1914 series of articles, *In the Cause of Architecture*, he wrote: "The style of the thing, therefore, will be the man; it is his. *Let his forms alone.*" Defending individualism, Wright thus associates style with the architect, rather than with the forms of his buildings. Le Corbusier, ever polemic, also challenged the notion of historical style when, in 1923, he said simply, "Styles are a lie." And in his book *Précisions* he expresses this point through a diagram, in which sketches representing the classical styles of the past are struck through in red and captioned: "Ceci n'est pas l'architecture, ce sont les styles." ("This is not architecture, these are styles.") Following suit in 1923, Mies van der Rohe writes in the review *G* (*Gestaltung*) which he himself edited: "Form as an aim is formalism; and that we reject. Neither do we aspire to a style." And, in 1935, Walter Gropius, referring to the Bauhaus teaching project, wrote: "The object of the Bauhaus was not to propagate any 'style,' system, dogma, formula or vogue, but to exert a revitalizing influence on design."[22] Saarinen, for his part, made a similar argument when, in conversation with a student in 1958, and in reference to federal architecture, he drew a distinction between spirit and style: "I have no objection to the classic spirit. For government buildings, such a spirit should prevail. But not the *style* or the *dilution* of the style. That is where the mistake is made."[23]

The statements of such influential figures amount to a total rejection of the very idea of style as an architectural endpoint. It is remarkable, then, that the term International Style, promoted by Johnson, Hitchcock, and Alfred H. Barr Jr. (of the Museum of Modern Art) is still used today to refer to their work. Johnson's influence was especially crucial in disseminating the term. Passionately interested in history, Johnson consciously aimed to impose a "new and lasting 'Great Style'" for the twentieth century that would be as powerful and iconic as the great styles of the past.[24] So, for example, he knowingly altered Mies's intentions by deliberately omitting the phrase "Neither do we aspire to a style" from the latter's statement in *G* magazine when including a translation of it in his 1947 monograph.

While in the plastic arts the term *style* has historically been associated with the forms an artist creates, linguistically, the term has long been connected directly to the author.[25] So we have Comte de Buffon's 1753 classical formulation, linking style to author—*Le style est l'homme même*. In addition to its formal significance, style can be understood as that which is different in the individual or unique to the manner and actions of a particular person. Style is thus linked to personal experience and to today's notion of signature, as Arthur Schopenhauer's 1851 formulation of style anticipated: "Style is the physiognomy of the mind."

Saarinen never hesitated to cite personal experience as a source of inspiration in his work. To design the nondenominational Chapel at Massachusetts Institute of Technology (1953–56), for example, he deliberately drew on a spiritual experience he had while traveling through Greece. Circular in plan, the chapel has a large skylight and additional perimeter lighting. "I have always remembered one night on my travels as a student when I sat in a mountain village in Sparta. There was bright moonlight over head and there was a soft, hushed secondary light around the horizon. That sort of bilateral lighting seemed best to achieve this other-worldly sense. Thus, the central light would come from above the altar—dramatized by the shimmering golden screen by Harry Bertoia—and the secondary light would be reflected up from the surrounding moat through the arches."[26]

"Style for the job," a phrase used derisively among architects during the 1950s and 1960s, describes Saarinen's design philosophy.[27] In associating "style" and "job," it limits the meaning of style by circumscribing it to a particular work. It also invokes the criterion of difference, in applying to each work a particular "style." Unlike the incoherent fragmentation suggested by "adhocism,"[28] another term that cropped up around the same time, "style for the job" conveyed the proud resolve of pragmatism. Each specific

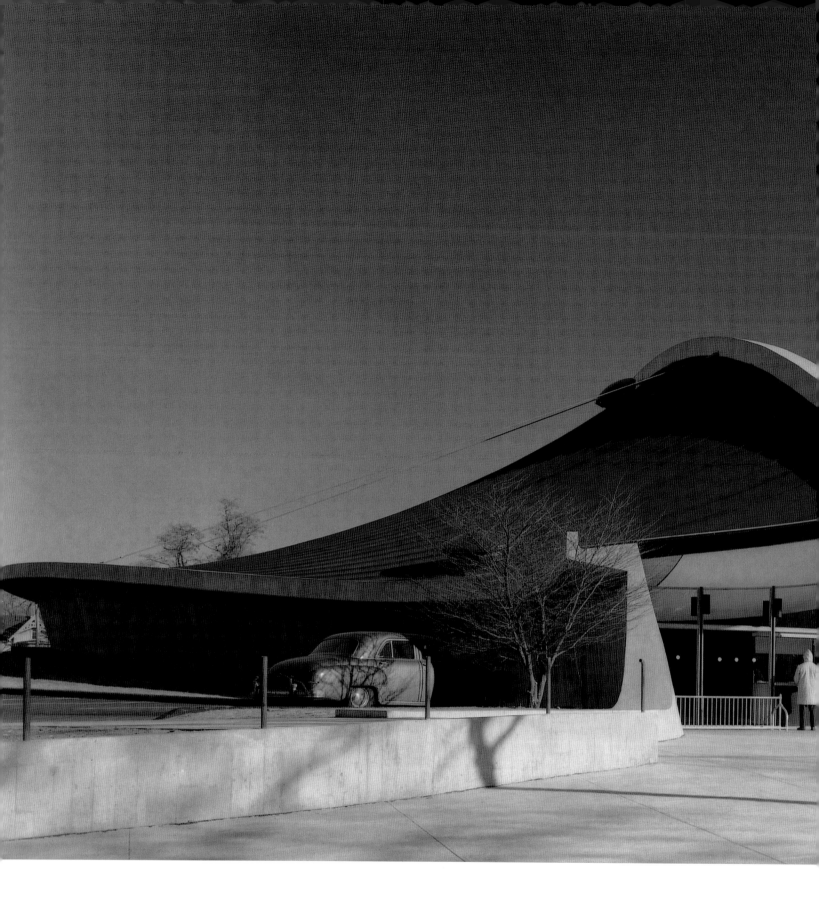

ABOVE AND FOLLOWING SPREAD Ingalls Hockey Rink, Yale University, New Haven, CT, 1953–59
Ezra Stoller © Esto

case is processed in a specific manner. What is appropriate for a hockey rink at Yale is not necessarily appropriate for the corporate headquarters of John Deere. The soaring sight lines designed to evoke fantasies of flight would have been ill-suited to the well-tempered needs of a broadcasting company's offices.

While this pragmatic approach made sense on a case-by-case basis, the cumulative effect was stylistic eclecticism, which, to most people, had a decidedly pejorative connotation, as it still does today. Yet Saarinen, like many of his contemporaries, viewed eclecticism as a necessary and noble response to the conditions of the period. This recalled traditional eclecticism, which was regarded as the culmination of academic achievement. In 1965, Peter Collins made this point as the guideline for his critique of architecure when he quoted Denis Diderot on the subject:

> An eclectic is a philosopher who tramples underfoot prejudice, tradition, seniority, universal consent, authority, and everything which subjugates mass opinion; who dares to think for himself, go back to the clearest general principles, examine them, discuss them, and accept nothing except on the evidence of his own experience and reason; and who, from all the philosophies which he has analyzed without respect to persons, and without partiality, makes a philosophy of his own, peculiar to himself.[29]

Saarinen's pragmatism parallels this formulation of eclecticism. Indeed, the diversity of his work, far from being seen in stylistic terms, should be understood as the product of a powerful creative force—the architect himself. As Saarinen wrote:

> It is on the individual, his sensitivities and understanding, that our whole success or failure rests. He must recognize that this is a new kind of civilization in which the artist will be used in a new and different way. The neat categories of bygone days do not hold true any longer. His job requires a curious combination of intuition and "crust." He must be sensitive and adaptable to trends and needs; he must be part of and understand our civilization. At the same time, he is not just a mirror; he is also a co-creator and must have the strength and urge to produce form, not compromise.[30]

Seen from this perspective, the diversity of Saarinen's work acquires a new dimension as a *multiplicity*. In contrast to other architects at the time, so intent on developing one single aspect of design, Eero Saarinen "wanted to embrace the entire body" when designing, something that in turn might lead to inquiry and indecision—witness for

ABOVE John Deere & Company Headquarters, Moline, IL, 1957–63. Saarinen (right) with model
FOLLOWING SPREADS Deere & Company Headquarters

instance painstakingly compiled charts of facts and figures he created for so many of the projects undertaken.[31] With his constant experimenting and self-evaluation, Saarinen clearly fits the aforementioned definition of an eclectic. As he said in an interview published in 1953 in the *New York Times*, anticipating present-day concerns in architecture, "In the end, you can only create and make decisions according to your own integrity."[32]

CREATING

I must admit that the statement my ego liked the most was "methodical but not cautious architect." That I liked especially.

Between the architect and the work of architecture lies that murky and often indecipherable terrain known as the creative process. Within the historiography of art—and, by extension, architecture—there has been, understandably, some reluctance to deal with this amorphous space, as it is generally regarded as little more than guesswork.[1] Nevertheless, modern art, especially conceptual art, has often incorporated the creative process within the work of art itself.

One intrepid individual who braved the terrain of creativity was American psychologist J. P. Guilford. In his seminal 1950 essay, "Creativity," Guilford attempted to define the study of creativity from a psychometric perspective. Critical of research that assumed the creative process to be a linear succession of phases (preparation, incubation, inspiration, and evaluation),[2] he designed a factor-analysis investigation involving criteria such as sensibility to problems, ideational fluency, flexibility, ideational novelty, synthesizing ability, analyzing ability, reorganizing and redefining ability, span of ideational structure, and evaluating ability. His model, which established a basis for evaluating the factors that contribute to a creative personality, became an essential reference for psychological studies of creativity.

In 1959, continuing in Guilford's line, Donald W. MacKinnon and Wallace B. Hall, psychologists at the Institute of Personality Assessment and Research in Berkeley, California, initiated a study designed to determine the characteristic traits of the creative personality. For their subjects they chose architects, because among various creative practices considered for study—creative writing, mathematics, industrial research, physical science, and engineering—architecture combined artistic and scientific creativity through diverse professional skills. And with the help of a panel of five professors, eleven editors from the major American architectural journals, and the group of invited architects themselves, forty architects regarded by the profession as creative, agreed to spend a weekend at the institute completing various creativity tests. Saarinen was a member of the group.

MacKinnon published the results of this study, sponsored in large part by the Carnegie Corporation, in a 1962 essay for *American Psychologist* entitled "The Nature and Nurture of Creative Talent." He detailed the assessment method, in which the subjects were organized into groups of ten and studied by various means, including:

> ... by problem solving experiments; by tests designed to discover what a person does not know or is unable or unwilling to reveal about himself; by tests and questionnaires that permit a person to manifest various aspects of his personality and to express his attitudes, interests, and values; by searching interviews that

cover the life history and reveal the present structure of the person; and by specially contrived social situations of a stressful character which call for the subject's best behavior in a socially defined role.[3]

Describing one specific exercise, the mosaic test, MacKinnon stated that the subjects were "presented with a large selection of one-inch squares of varicolored posterboard and asked to construct, within a thirty-minute period, a pleasing, completely filled-in 8 x 10-inch mosaic." From the twenty-two available colors, he noted that some architects made order out of the largest possible number of colors, while others selected the fewest colors possible, and "one used only one color, all white."[4] Although MacKinnon had scrupulously kept the participants' identities anonymous in his report, after they had all finished the test in the booths, Saarinen revealed to Philip Johnson, who was another of the forty guinea pigs, how he had solved the problem:

> I asked Philip what he did with the tiles, and he said, "Oh, those colors were awful.
> I threw the colored tiles away and used only the black and white. What did you do,
> Eero?"—I told Philip I had used only the white, and he was so jealous.[5]

Curiously, MacKinnon and Hall had established a link between the responses in which the greatest number of colors had been selected and the participants with the highest level of creativity. Thus, despite being considered by his peers to be one of the most creative architects, Saarinen received the lowest possible score for creativity on the mosaic test. (In fact, their supposed correspondence between creativity and the variety of color selection was borne out in just 38 percent of the cases.)

In view of his body of work, Saarinen's single-color solution to the mosaic test is revealing. While the selection of one color only seems anathema to the variety of structures and forms he designed over the years, in fact, whenever he was presented with maximum creative freedom, Saarinen always chose the equivalent of one single color: "I have come to the conviction that once one embarks on a concept for a building, this concept has to be exaggerated and overstated and repeated in every part of its interior, so that wherever you are, inside or outside, the building sings with the same message."[6] Choosing all white for his mosaic perfectly reflects one of Saarinen's characteristics, his pursuit of unity in each of his buildings.

Among the defining traits of the creative architect, MacKinnon concluded that intuition ranked high. A person tending toward intuitive perception, as opposed to sense perception, he said, "looks expectantly for a bridge or link between that which is given

and present and that which is not yet thought of, focusing habitually upon possibilities."
Saarinen was keenly aware of the importance of intuition and comfortable relying on his
own. In a 1959 interview published in *Horizon* magazine, he acknowledged that "intuition plays a large part in architecture, because we don't have an IBM machine big
enough to take all the factors into consideration. So, you depend on intuition. But, boy!
Wherever you can apply straight thinking or IBM machine methods or things like that,
you absolutely have to do it." To forecast, in 1959, the possibility of the widespread
use of computers suggests another aspect of Saarinen's acute intuitive ability and
adaptability to new technology. Of course, as the architect of complexes for IBM
in Rochester and Yorktown, New York (1956–59 and 1957–61, respectively), he was
certainly familiar with developments in the computer industry.[7]

In 1952 Saarinen told a friend: "The only architecture which interests me is architecture as a fine art. That is what I want to pursue." This predilection for the artistic
is another chief characteristic of the architect's creative personality according to
MacKinnon's assessment. Like certain mathematicians, for whom the laws pertaining
to numbers have an intrinsic beauty indescribable to those outside the field, Saarinen's
aestheticism transcended the visual. He appreciated the beauty in the functional or
constructive relations of each project, and reveled in the operational elegance of
design possibilities. "I think sometimes architecture is like a marvelous three-dimensional chess game. Every move or decision affects every other move and decision,"
he said to a student in 1960.[8]

It's not surprising, given his understanding of the importance of intuition and the
innovation it engenders, that Saarinen put great stock in the individual, where he identified the key to failure or success. He understood this individuality in a wide sense:
"Great architecture is both universal and individual," he said in a 1956 address.[9]
Saarinen expanded on individuality, indicating that for him architecture is universal as
an expression of an epoch and individual as an expression of the philosophy of the
individual. The diversity in his architectural oeuvre demonstrates how seriously he took
this belief. Every one of his projects involved unique ways of approaching the given
challenges in extremely varied contexts.

If he was intuitive, artistic, and individualistic, Saarinen was not at all whimsical.
He had a fierce competitive streak and a pronounced fixation on success that kept
him intently focused on building a career. The desire for stardom was seldom overtly
acknowledged in the understated echelon of an architectural practice, but Saarinen
openly confessed his concern for distinction: "I admit frankly I would like a place in
architectural history." Recognition, for him, depended not only on talent but also on

hard work. From his student days at Yale, he distinguished himself by winning academic honors including the Beaux-Arts competitions—many in a row—and taking great pride in defeating his competitors. Throughout his career he entered and won architectural competitions—at a time when they were not so commonplace as they are today. Even in his early years in his father's studio, colleagues remarked on a discernible climate of competitiveness. His individual participation in the Jefferson National Expansion Memorial competition in 1947 was a direct challenge to his father. Saarinen clearly recognized his own filial power struggle. In 1952, just two years after Eliel's death, he offered the heartfelt observation, "Now that I have achieved success and the 'competition' with my father has ended, a yearning has come for a more rounded life."[10]

The competitor in him did not go unnoticed by his contemporaries. In an article entitled "Eero Saarinen: A Complete Architect," architecture critic Walter McQuade profiled Saarinen, describing him as having the nature of a "competitor and cooperator." Similarly, Kevin Roche describes him as "a very competitive person. In a meeting he always wanted to win, whatever it was, whatever the subject might be, he wanted to win. Everything was a challenge." Roche recognized that competitiveness was just one facet of Saarinen's creative personality and by no means the defining feature: "He had an extraordinary character, in the sense that he was, as many people would say, an absolutely consummate architect, totally absorbed by the design process, more than anybody I've ever met or seen."[11]

Other colleagues and commentators saw his determination as a mark of genius. They recognized that, as opposed to genius based purely on talent or inspiration, Saarinen's was rooted in his steadfast drive and willingness to work and rework a problem—indeed, it was not uncommon for him to significantly change a project that was virtually completed. Designer and architect Charles Eames, a friend at Cranbrook who later collaborated with Saarinen on design projects, described him as a "genius in whom you can see the gears working because they are on the outside." Cesar Pelli, who spent ten years in Saarinen's office, says: "Eero did not seek to be a genius or to have all the answers, but he was ready to roll his sleeves up, to worry. He exhibited all his faults. He allowed one to collaborate with him, to correct him. We continually criticized him, which really helped demythicize the process of design."[12]

"Methodical but not cautious" was the description Saarinen said his "ego liked the most." He appreciated the way it synthesized his technical and artistic ambitions, without privileging one over the other. And he felt that it perfectly captured the humanist ideal—an ideal he was forever striving to embody. The handwritten text dated April 1952,

ABOVE Watson Research Center, IBM, Yorktown, NY, 1957–61

when his first marriage was in crisis, illustrates his ever-present impulse towards self-improvement. After taking stock of his life and setting himself some guidelines to follow, he then proposes various ways he could develop and expand, including: developing himself as a warmer, more generous, more enthusiastic human being; cultivating new friendships in the artistic world; traveling in Japan, Mexico, Greece, and Europe; creating his own home after Hvitträsk; adding to skiing and swimming hobbies such as music, history, philosophy, literature; and taking an active interest in architectural education.[13]

In addition to providing clues to his personal preferences, this text illustrates his penchant for self-reflection—another characteristic of the creative Saarinen. His willingness to explore the maximum number of possibilities he could imagine for his own self-improvement—a pursuit that sometimes took him to the point of indecision—parallels the way in which he approached his projects. If it is possible to talk about psychological types in architects, one might include Eero Saarinen in the category of those who pursue many objectives but believe that they relate everything to a central vision. In this context, Saarinen aligned himself with Le Corbusier, writing: "My belief is sincerely that we must explore and expand the horizons of our architecture. In this sense, I align myself humbly with Le Corbusier and against Mies van der Rohe, although I admire his achievements immensely."[14]

THE TWA TERMINAL
QUEENS, NEW YORK
1956–62

Explore and expand he did. In February 1956, upon receiving the commission from Trans World Airlines president Ralph S. Damon for the company's new terminal at Idlewild, Saarinen began a process of creative experimentation that would ultimately result in one of the most revolutionary architectural statements of the period.

With an established reputation, especially after undertaking as sizable a project as the General Motors Technical Center, Saarinen's office was engaged in fifteen other projects at the time. He and his colleagues immediately started collecting data on planes and passengers, and elaborating charts and checklists of their findings, something he had already done at the Office of Strategic Services. As Kevin Roche recalls, "We would travel to airports and time planes taking on passengers, taking off and landing, the time it took to go from the sidewalk to ticketing, checking-in your baggage, stopwatch timing all those things." Similar information was collected at New York's Grand Central Terminal, which had the highest passenger flow of any station in the United States at that time, with up to 250,000 passengers on peak days, and was the perfect place to time and study passenger movement. There, Saarinen and his staff discovered that foot traffic did not follow rectilinear lines. On the contrary, upon meeting an obstacle, people pursued curved paths, unconsciously observing laws similar to those of aerodynamics. According to Roche, these observations led directly to the rounded, pseudo-triangular form of the TWA plan.[15]

The terminal's curved plan was also a response to the building's site. One of the two primary objectives Saarinen outlined in his initial project statement was to create a signature terminal that would provide a distinctive identity for the airline within the context of the airport's other structures. "Its particular site—directly opposite Idlewild's main entrance road and at the apex of the curve in the far end of the terminal complex—gave us the opportunity of designing a building that could relate to the surrounding in mass but still assert itself as a dramatic accent," Saarinen wrote in the 1959 project statement.

One of his first attempts at addressing the site's specificity was captured on the back of a menu. Shortly after Saarinen himself appeared on the cover of *Time* magazine in July 1956, Eero and Aline Saarinen had dinner with Cranston Jones, associate editor of the magazine. When Jones asked Saarinen what he had in mind for the TWA building, Saarinen, who "habitually talked with a pencil....turned over the menu and began explaining his first ideas on the TWA Terminal—the concept, the plan, the site at Idlewild, the square footage," reported his wife, Aline.[16] He drew an impromptu plan showing the passenger flow, from entrance to extremities, following a curved trajectory—its triangular form is not yet defined, which demonstrates that the sketch was

truly one of the first diagrams. One perspective in particular shows Saarinen's concern for the conditions of the site, indicating how the projected building would adapt to the bend in the road, making a dramatic appearance.

Thus Saarinen's other principal objective—"to design a building in which the architecture itself would express the drama and specialness and excitement of travel"[17]—was also evident in the shell-like roofline he scrawled on the back of that menu. Its swooping, uplifted form was specifically intended to convey a feeling of motion and lightness.

As expressive as his sketches were, the TWA Terminal design was developed primarily through models rather than drawings. The Beaux-Arts tradition—from which many of today's architects would not be completely detached—placed the emphasis on drawing. Nearly every design was supposed to begin with plans, from which models could subsequently be made. The TWA project constitutes a unique case in contemporary architecture, perhaps the first one documented in which the inverse procedure was followed: First they built models and then they used the small structures to elaborate drawings.

The very first working model was built in Saarinen's office toward the end of 1956, at an aproximate scale of 1 inch to 4 feet (1:50). In a photograph taken around that time, Saarinen and Roche are in the Bloomfield Hills office trying out a solution with some ribs for the shell, which involved a shape similar to the one Saarinen had designed a few years earlier for Kresge Auditorium at MIT. Some time later, after returning from Australia, where he had gone to help judge the Sydney Opera House competition, resolved on 29 January 1957, Saarinen built a model that Kevin Roche likened to a helmet, for its rounded and pitched form, and related to the competition. "Yes, I think we might say there is an influence from it: an earlier model that Eero did after he came back from Sydney had a more pronounced Nordic helmet type shape, or actually more of a Spanish helmet, a kind of conquistador." The introduction of an elevated shell ridge into the scheme is the most obvious difference between the first and second models. Much has been written about whether Jørn Utzon's award-winning design for Sydney influenced Saarinen's concept for TWA, as the conquistador model might suggest, or whether, conversely, Utzon's form was inspired by similar-shaped buildings—the Kresge Auditorium, for example—that Saarinen had already designed. With its distinctive convex roof, the form of which constituted one-eighth of a sphere, the Kresge building, completed in 1955, may have informed the slivered shell shapes Utzon proposed for Sydney.[18]

Another unique document—to which Peter Papademetriou has called attention—is a cluster of pencil sketches of the terminal roof that Saarinen doodled on the top of his April 1957 desk calendar.[19] This too provides evidence of Utzon's influence on the

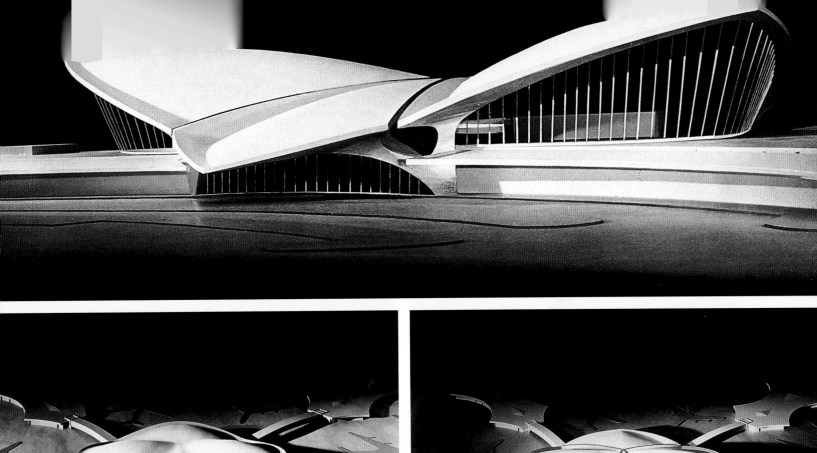
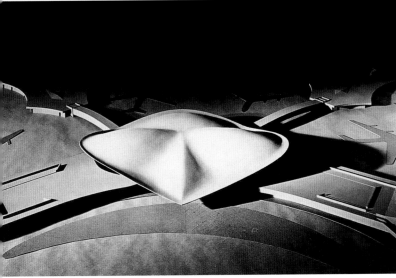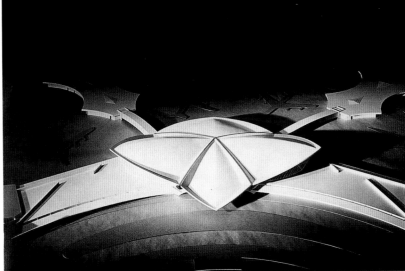

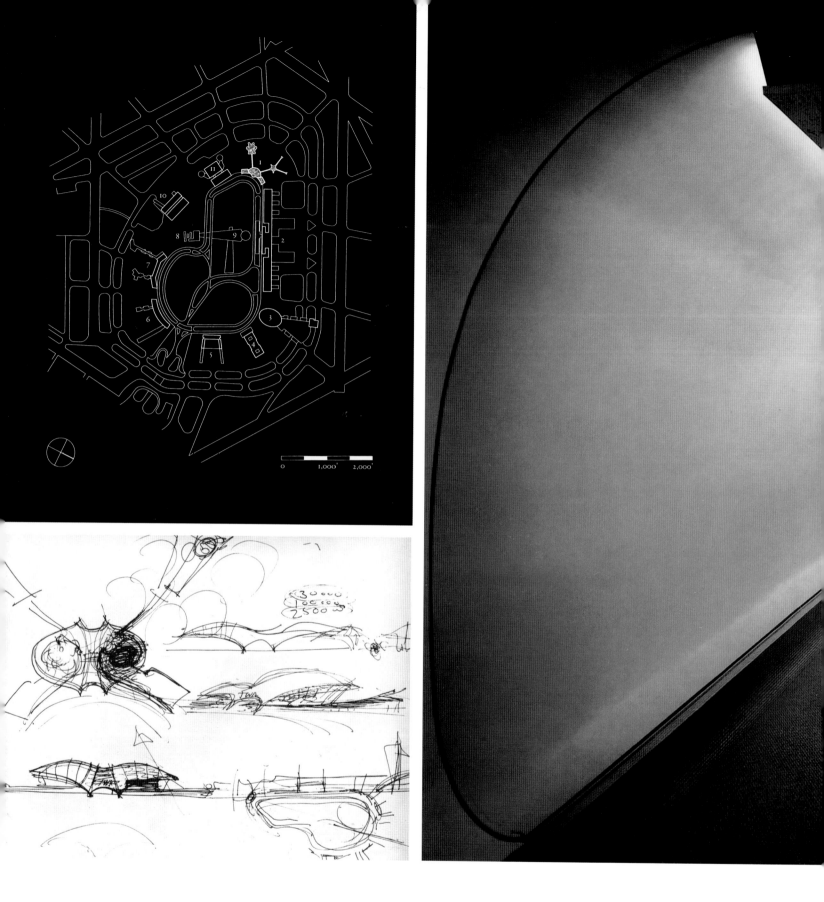

TOP LEFT TWA Terminal, Queens, NY, 1956–62. Master plan
BOTTOM LEFT TWA Terminal. Saarinen sketches
RIGHT TWA Terminal. Ezra Stoller © Esto

TWA project. The loose-lined drawings depict various structural options: a four-vault solution in which the segments are joined in a central point, a rounded form involving curved panels, and several hoodlike shapes that presage the building's final form. At least two bear a striking resemblance to the curved series of pointed eaves Utzon had shown in his competition-winning design just three months before.

Subsequent models, produced by professional model-makers at a scale of approximately 1 inch to 16 feet (1:200), reveal two intermediate stages between the continuous dorsal shape of the first design and the final form that was built.[20] The first stage resembles the perspective Saarinen sketched for Cranston Jones. The next one reveals a rounder, more unitary structure, before the ceiling vaults were separated and the angular lines of the roof became so pronounced. In the final model the vaults are distinctly separate, their jutting, diamond-shaped contours joined on two sides to form a four-pointed star. The three models illustrate Saarinen's ongoing effort to resolve one particular problem: to reduce the exceptionally thick edge of the beam that would be needed to support the length and height of the cantilever. The four-vault structure, like the one he sketched in the margins of his desk calendar, was the solution that was developed by the engineers at Ammann & Whitney.

Another account of how Saarinen conceived the four-vault solution is the legendary grapefruit story. As Roche tells it: "Eero was eating breakfast one morning and was using the rind of his grapefruit to describe the terminal shell. He pushed down its center to mimic the depression that he desired, and the grapefruit bulged. This was the seed for the four bulges of the shell."[21] Evidently, inspiration could strike anywhere and at any time.

One such place was Cranbrook, used many times as a model. As Cesar Pelli recalls: "We continuously used Cranbrook as a reference point, the buildings, the space between the buildings—not as architecture, but as a relation of forms, or relation of elements, of volumes and spaces." Another source of inspiration for TWA was the Lambert Airport terminal in St. Louis. Designed by Leinweber, Yamasaki, and Hellmuth, the terminal opened in 1956, right around the time Saarinen received the commission from TWA. Architect Minoru Yamasaki, who was a close friend of Saarinen's, endowed the structure with a soaring glass-shell roof reminiscent of a vaulted type common to Roman baths. Upon its completion, it was the first contemporary air terminal to incorporate the sort of grand space typical of the railway stations built in the nineteenth century. The terminal's central rectangular space, which encompasses three square-based vaults, measures 120 by 400 feet, with a maximum height of 32 feet. By comparison, the vaulted space of the TWA Terminal measures 213 by 360 feet, with a maximum

height of 55 feet. While formal similarities between the two buildings are probably coincidental, both Kevin Roche and Cesar Pelli cite Lambert as a significant influence on the large space of the TWA Terminal.[22]

Two other places that surely inspired Saarinen's terminal design were the Helsinki Railway Station, built by Eliel Saarinen in 1914, and McKim, Mead and White's Pennsylvania Station, which opened in New York City in 1910. With its considerable proportions and elaborated interior, the Helsinki station endowed the city with the sort of grandeur Eliel had observed on his research trips to the principal railway stations of England, Scotland, and Germany. For Eero Saarinen, that same sense of grandeur was palpable in Penn Station's central space. Measuring 100 by 270 feet, with a height of 145 feet, its lofty, light-filled interior was typologically influenced by Roman thermal baths, as art historian Nikolaus Pevsner has demonstrated. In the TWA Terminal, Saarinen pursued a twofold objective: an appearance of lightness and a sensation akin to that one might experience in the interior of a Roman bath. By 1961 his comparison to the Roman baths took on a somewhat different connotation: "TWA is beginning to look marvelous," he said. "If anything happened and they had to stop work right now and just leave it in this state, I think it would make a beautiful ruin, like the Baths of Caracalla."[23]

The final working model for the TWA Terminal was built in the second half of 1957 at a scale of approximately 1 inch to 2 feet (1:25). Its unusually generous size enabled Saarinen and his colleagues to work three-dimensionally. They could insert and remove various elements and experiment with different structural possibilities, all the while enjoying a clear perspective of the building as a whole—something that was especially important to Saarinen, who relied heavily on visual observation. Typically, the design team would meet at the model shop, develop a new shape, place it on the model, and test the effect. Then, if necessary, the shape would be modified. Essentially a trial-and-error system, this methodology helped the designers anticipate problems by allowing them to encounter the unexpected before seeing it constructed.[24]

For Saarinen, who had trained as a sculptor before turning to architecture, tactile interaction with his design was an essential part of the creative process. It was only after an ideal had been worked out in model format that he felt capable of proceeding with drawn plans: "One of the happiest days was after we had worked out the supports in model form. Finally we were able to make drawings of what we actually had. In these drawings we found that the support plans were marvelous-looking things, showing forms that could never have been arrived at on paper." Pelli, who was responsible for this support solution, recalls that he started with a three-dimensional scheme of steel reinforcement precisely because it enabled him to consider the structural behavior of the supports. The working model was not only useful in the discussions between architects, office staff, collaborators, and clients; it was also a perfect tool for simulating interior spaces and the effects that space and light would have on the passengers using the terminal. In some projects Saarinen even extended this testing to constructed procedures and effects (for the Deere & Company headquarters in Moline, Illinois, 1956–63, he built a mock-up of the facade to check the weathering behavior of corrosion-resistant Corten steel, then a new material used in architecture).[25]

The formal complexity of the TWA Terminal was reflected in the great number of subsequent drawings made to produce it. Out of the nearly six hundred made in the design development phase, about two hundred refer to the structure that was actually built. And the difficult process of translating the form from model to drawing paralleled the trials of transferring the working drawings to the site and to formwork. The construction company, Grove Shepherd Wilson & Kruge, made the formwork study following sections at 1-foot intervals to fit the intricacies of the curved surfaces. By 1960, about midway through construction, the intricacies of the site work required the builders to turn in part to computer-generated computations.[26]

Saarinen's work with models on the TWA Terminal demonstrates the importance of the process-of-making rather than mere project-drawing. Working with models, with a methodology based more upon *bricolage* than projection through drawing, allowed for unexpected results, and this explains the complexities of the forms in the finished building. In this respect Saarinen's results differ from those of expressionists like Eric Mendelsohn, and his process, at least in the case of TWA, is closer to being a precedent for present-day architects such as Frank Gehry,) who design through an extensive modeling process.

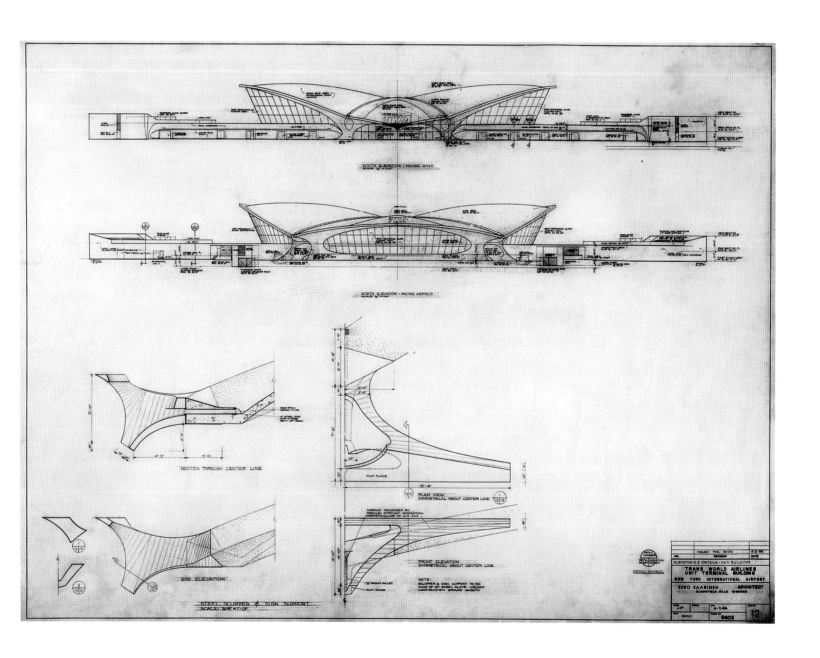

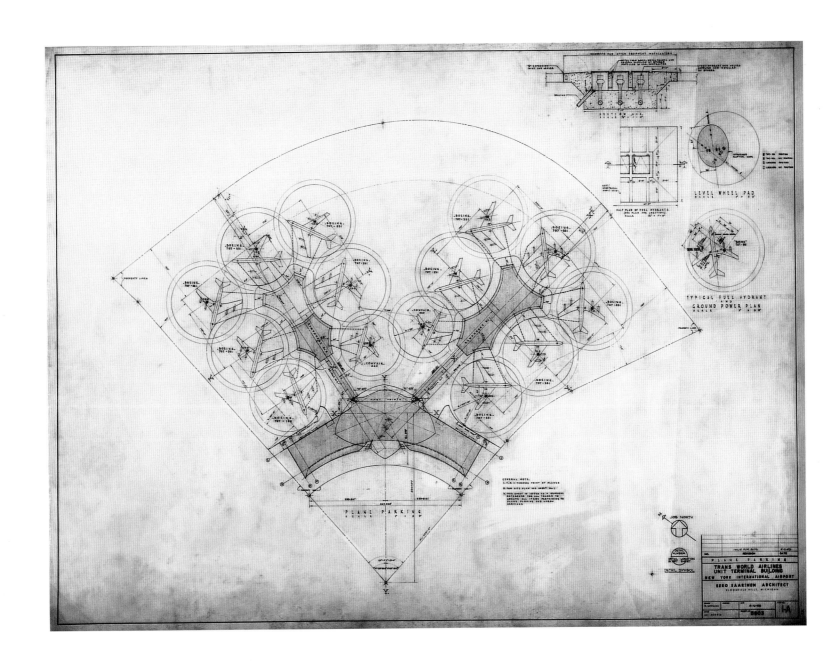

LEFT TWA Terminal, Queens, NY, 1956–62. Elevations and details

ABOVE TWA Terminal. Airplane-positioning diagram

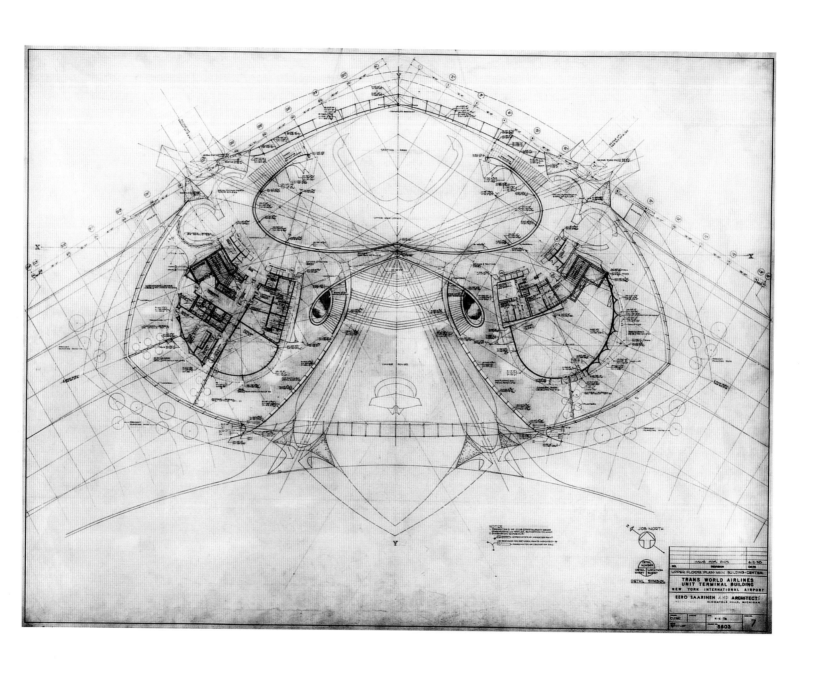

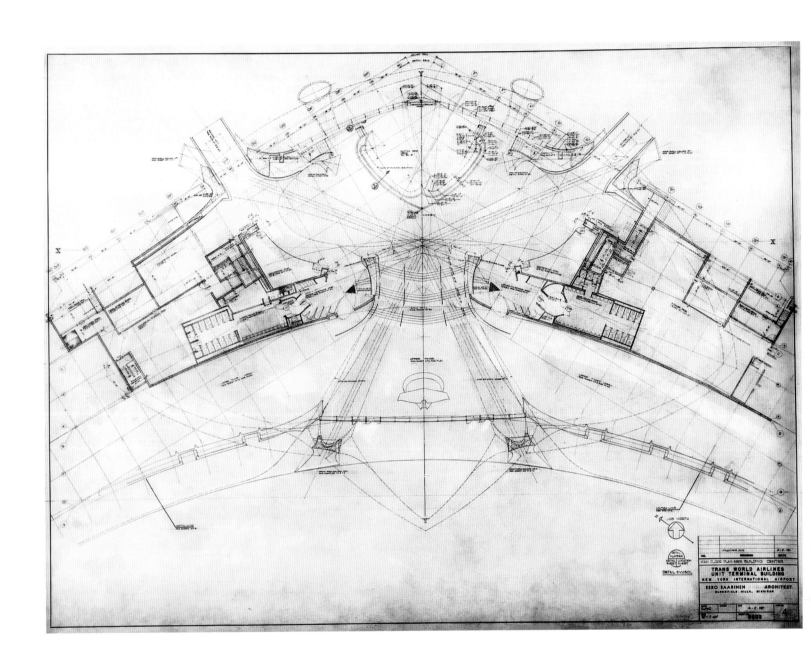

LEFT TWA Terminal, Queens, NY, 1956–62. Upper-floor plan

ABOVE TWA Terminal. Main-floor plan

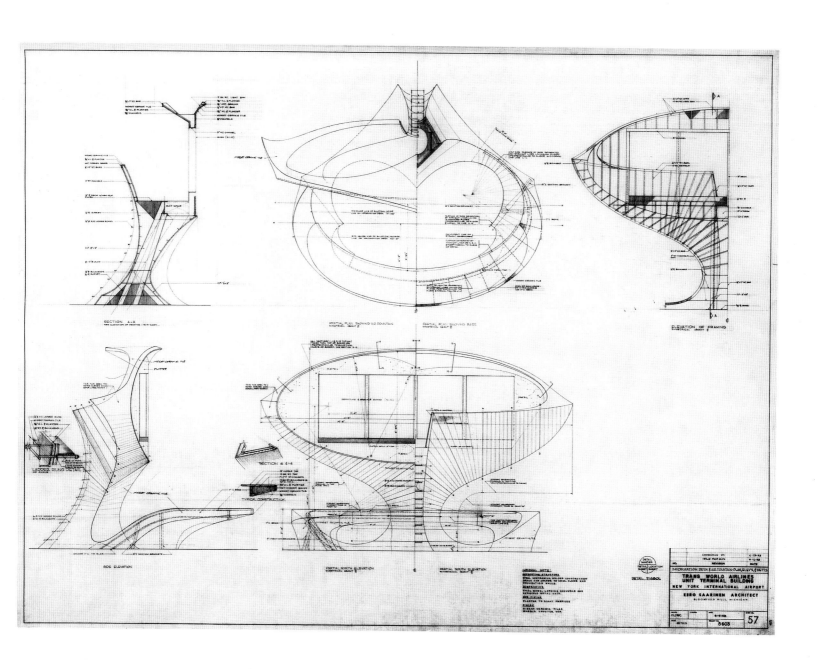

SECTION A-A

PARTIAL PLAN SHOWING KID FOUNTAIN

PARTIAL PLAN SHOWING RAMP

ELEVATION OF FRAMING

SIDE ELEVATION

SECTION B & C

TYPICAL CONSTRUCTION

PARTIAL NORTH ELEVATION

PARTIAL SOUTH ELEVATION

DETAIL SYMBOL

GENERAL NOTE:

TRANS WORLD AIRLINES
UNIT TERMINAL BUILDING
NEW YORK INTERNATIONAL AIRPORT

EERO SAARINEN ARCHITECT
BLOOMFIELD HILLS, MICHIGAN

57

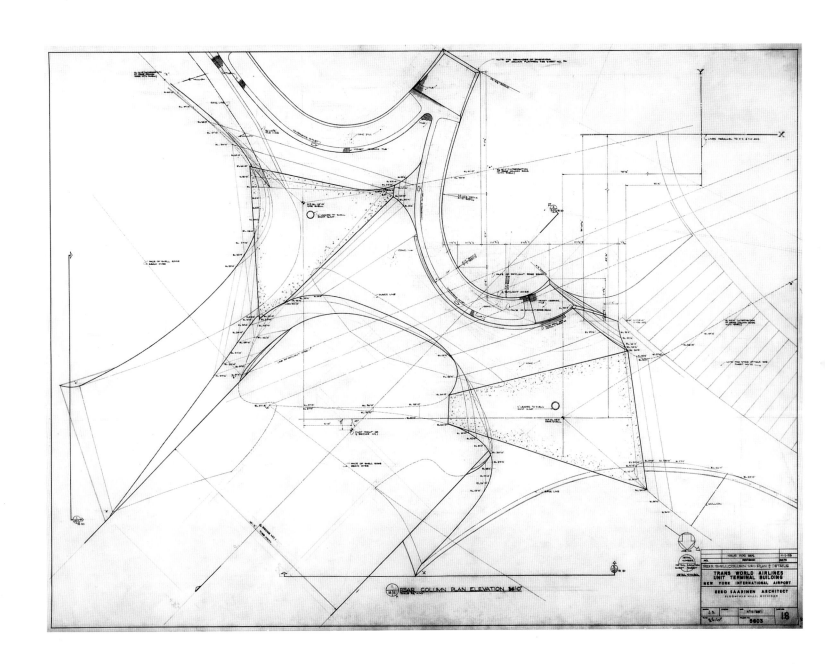

When the terminal finally opened in 1962—just a year after Saarinen had suddenly died—only one of its two flight wings was complete (the second was not completed until 1970), but its eye-catching futurism captivated the public imagination. Critical response ranged from enchantment to outrage. The architectural press for the most part reviewed it favorably. *Architectural Forum*, for example, praised the terminal, describing both process and project as graceful, inventive, and sculptural in its regular coverage of the design. On the other hand, influential scholar Vincent Scully railed against Saarinen's tendency to use whammo shapes in a critique that can only be described as hostile.[27]

In his monograph on Saarinen—published just after Saarinen's death—Allan Temko, art and architecture critic for the *San Francisco Chronicle*, presented a somewhat more balanced evaluation. He called the design "one of the most electrifying to be published in the late fifties," but also remarked that "its eloquence seems too rich for the content of the problem and in the context of its surroundings." And while he ultimately condemned the project for its instantaneous obsolescence, he recognized that it was as much society's fault as Saarinen's: "TWA's failure, then, was part of much broader failings of our irrationally driven society. Idlewild—as Saarinen came to know better than anyone else long before TWA's completion—was predicated on wrong notions of architectural and operational rivalry."[28]

Other critics voiced similar concerns about the building's adaptability, specifically about whether it could accommodate the airport's ever-changing needs. For architectural critic Reyner Banham, the terminal's practical drawbacks, which reflected an unclear relation between function and symbol, were no more egregious than those of other airport buildings. In his view, the problem was that the aeronautics industry was continually creating new aircraft to respond to new needs, and that the airport infrastructure simply couldn't keep up. In an essay titled "The Obsolescent Airport" he wrote, "airports have proven to be the most transitional and transient building types of our time, always unfinished, always out of date."[29]

One of the most technically qualified critiques came from Italian engineer Pier Luigi Nervi, who by 1955 already had a solid reputation in the United States. Nervi considered the terminal "too heavy and elaborate for the problem it seeks to solve."[30] As an engineer, Nervi was concerned, above all, with the optimization of material and formal simplicity. He felt that the TWA shells, which were designed by the engineering firm of Ammann & Whitney to eliminate deflection problems by ranging in thickness from 6 to 36 inches, were a conservative structural design that impaired the overall effectiveness of the concept.

Many critics associated the terminal's form with a bird spreading its wings. Saarinen himself described his first proposal for the terminal as "pigeon-toed" and later referred to the building as a "Leonardo da Vinci flying machine." Publicly, however, he maintained that any association between his design and any sort of winged creature was purely unintentional. "The fact that to some people it looked like a bird in flight was really coincidental. That was the last thing we ever thought about,"he wrote in the project statement in 1962. And in an early draft for this statement he openly stated that "any resemblance to anything other than a piece of architecture is purely in the eye of the beholder or in the editorializing of the 'trend-makers.'"[31]

Saarinen's disavowal of this obvious association represents a more general rejection of imitation and popular symbolism—indeed, Saarinen asserted that the terminal used "completely new vocabularies." But for Robert Venturi, who would soon launch his seminal postmodern discourse, it was precisely in Saarinen's figurative vocabulary, seen as a weakness at the time, that his enormous relevance lay. "It [his vocabulary] was a result of his thinking of his buildings, his architecture as evolving from vocabulary rather than from function, or from a kind of simple system, rather than straight out of function which was the modern idea."[32]

By his own account, Saarinen's approach was expressionistic, frequently compared to Eric Mendelsohn and to neo-expressionists such as Hans Scharoun, Jørn Utzon, and Oscar Niemeyer. This association with expressionism leads us beyond a strict modernism to the tradition of architecture parlante. A late-eighteenth-century conception, architecture parlante was an "active architecture" that sought to produce a reaction in the spectator. Notions of character and expression were central to its nature, as articulated by Étienne-Louis Boullée, one of its principal practitioners: "What I call giving character to a piece of work is the art of employing in any production all the means that belong and are relative to the subject in question, so that the spectator does not experience any sentiment other than those the subject ought to inspire, that are essential to him and which he is capable of feeling."[33] More than 150 years later, in a lecture at Dickinson College, Saarinen described his own strategy in remarkably similar terms:

> When I approach an architectural problem, I try to think out the real significance of the problem. What is the essence and how can the total structure capture that essence? How can the whole building convey emotionally the purpose and meaning of the building? Conveying significant meaning is part of the inspirational purpose of architecture and, therefore, for me, it is a fundamental principle of our art.[34]

In the TWA Terminal, Saarinen took the passenger's impression and experience to the limit. The idea was that wherever he went in the terminal, the passenger would be able to sense the excitement of travel. Whether he was approaching the information desk, wandering around the central space, conversing at the check-in counter, or waiting in the lounge area, the passenger's experience would consistently evoke the wonder of flight. All the interior spaces employed the same formal vocabulary that Saarinen introduced in the exterior. From the tunnels leading to the boarding gates to the baggage claim areas to the footbridge between the mezzanines, the curved shape is present in every detail.

In a 1960 article for *Horizon,* Saarinen related these aspects of the terminal to the historical context of the baroque: "That's right, the baroque architects were wrestling with the same problem of creating dynamic space. Within the limits of the classical order and their technology, they were trying to see how far they could go into a nonstatic architecture. At TWA, we tried to take the discipline imposed by the concrete shell vault and give it nonstatic quality." Historian Henry-Russell Hitchcock also suggested Saarinen's association with the baroque. Hitchcock drew a parallel, which he recognized as somewhat dubious, between mid-twentieth-century modernism—he ended his historical account with Saarinen—and mannerist Italy; thus, he wondered about the possible arrival of "a vital new creation...as was the baroque around 1600."[35]

The exterior of the TWA Terminal was landmarked in 1994, but this did little to stem the deterioration of the building. With TWA now out of business, the Port Authority of New York and New Jersey, which controls the building, has planned a new terminal to be built alongside and connected to the Saarinen building. The possible mutilation of the TWA Terminal—and in particular its two flight wings—has triggered a heated reaction within the architectural community. The historical value of the building demands its preservation, while its obsolescence requires a new use so that it can be exploited in a suitable way. Practical considerations should be seen in the context of the importance of Saarinen's terminal as a symbol of contemporary architecture.

A few years prior to construction of the terminal, Le Corbusier designed the chapel of Notre-Dame-du-Haut, in Ronchamp, France (1950–55), one of the masterworks of modern architecture. There, he explored the sculptural and pictorial terrain, the freedom implicit in architectural modernism. The TWA Terminal is comparable to Ronchamp in this quest for expressive freedom, and is perhaps unique in its integration of function, structure, and expression. Any alterations to the terminal must be sensitive to the building's enormous value to contemporary architecture.

PREVIOUS SPREAD AND LEFT TWA Terminal, Queens, NY, 1956–62. Ezra Stoller © Esto

DWELLING

So, to the question, what is the purpose of architecture, I would answer: To shelter and enhance man's life on earth and to fulfill his beliefs in the nobility of his existence.

What is the origin of architecture? This is a question that has often been posed by architects. Some, entering the realm of the philosophical, have found an answer in the notion of inhabitation. In his essay "Building, Dwelling, Thinking," philosopher Martin Heidegger associated the three concepts, deriving architecture from the act of inhabitation: "Only if we are capable of dwelling, only then can we build," he wrote.[1] Saarinen, too, saw architecture as rooted in the concept of shelter, associating it with human existence and refusing to divorce it from local context: "a building grows from its site," he said.

Saarinen's profound interest in the relationship between architecture and inhabitation was rarely focused on the house, our most basic form of dwelling. Single-family homes are virtually absent from his body of work. Among the few homes he did design, the most significant was the 1958 Miller House in Columbus, Indiana, although his commitment to the design was limited.[2] Its living room, around which four distinct nodes—for parents, children, guests and servants, and service—were organized, was the nucleus of the house and featured a sunken, square conversation pit, something Saarinen had devised in one of his early competitions. Without completely rejecting the modernist open plan, Saarinen's design enclosed the spaces of these nodes around a fluid central space, a reference to the controlled open spaces he so admired in Japanese houses.

Precedents for the Miller residence can be found in the 1950 Entenza House, also known as Case Study House #9. This house was designed by Saarinen in collaboration with Charles Eames, who had been a friend since they met when Eames came to study at Cranbrook, before they went on to serve together as design instructors at the school. Part of Arts & Architecture magazine editor John Entenza's 1945 initiative to create alternative housing in Southern California, the Entenza House, a square-shaped, single-occupancy dwelling, comprised simply a central living space with a lounge pit flanked by service and bedroom areas. For Entenza, who occupied the house himself until 1955, the efficient, modular design represented an ideal response to his call for "space used elastically where many or few people can be accommodated." Many of the essential elements in the Entenza House had been developed by Saarinen, together with Oliver Lundquist, in their Pre-Assembled Compact (PAC) House—two prefabricated units in combination with an optional outdoor space—a winning proposal for the 1943 Designs for Postwar Living competition, also sponsored by Arts & Architecture.[3]

The Entenza House was actually one of two neighboring dwellings Eames and Saarinen devised together for the magazine's Case Study program. For Case Study House #8, which was designed for a couple, Saarinen's main contribution grew from

ABOVE AND RIGHT Irwin Miller House, Columbus, IN, 1953–57. Ezra Stoller © Esto

ABOVE AND RIGHT Charles Eames and Eero Saarinen, Entenza House, Case Study House #9, Santa Monica, CA, 1945–49

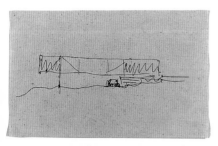

his 1945 Bridge House proposal (itself the product of a 1941 Community House design). After a complete redesign by Charles and Ray Eames—surely inspired by Mies van der Rohe's sketch of a glass house on a hillside—it became the Eames's own well known steel-framed residence.[4]

The Miller and Entenza houses are the only two documented examples of residences Saarinen ever built. The fact that houses played such a secondary role in his body of work was not due to a lack of commissions or time. Single-family home design simply did not fit into Saarinen's practice. The following statement, recorded in a 1958 interview by architect John Peter, makes his position clear:

> The house isn't really architecture. I think it's been too much overblown and much too important. Let's sort of relate this to other things. Now we know that the family is not as strong as [it] used to be. It's not as strong as an educational element. The education that children got through the family was much greater in earlier days than [it] is today. Yet the house as a piece of architecture has become terribly important. It really wasn't until the Victorian times....But lots of civilizations have lived with the house being an unimportant part, an anonymous part of architecture.[5]

This discourse, which relegated the practice of home design to the realm of irrelevance, ran counter to the modernist emphasis on the single-family dwelling, and demonstrated Saarinen's commitment to a broader idea of inhabitation. Indeed, early modern ideas about the house and its place in society, codified by the Congrès Internationaux d'Architecture Moderne (CIAM) in its functional Athens Charter of 1933, were just coming open to challenge. In the 1950s, a group of progressive Europeans led by Peter and Alison Smithson, known as Team 10, called for a radical departure from the modernist vision, replacing the idea of functional inhabitation with "cluster" habitats—"any coming together"—that broke with precedent and offered new forms for human relationships.[6]

Like his contemporaries in Team 10, Saarinen implicitly understood the significance of clustering. As a guiding concept it enabled him to consider spatial organization without relying on preconceived typologies, to find a frame of reference for contemporary forms of inhabitation without relation to the house. This is apparent in the TWA Terminal, where he suggests a kind of inhabitation even in the transitory nomadism of plane travel. For example, Saarinen designed way-finding schema that permit travelers to locate themselves and others in the terminal's unfamiliar terrain, and incorporated

TOP Mies van der Rohe. Glass house on a hillside, 1934. The Museum of Modern Art
MIDDLE Unfolding House project, 1945
BOTTOM Charles Eames and Eero Saarinen. Case Study houses #8 and 9, *Arts & Architecture*, December 1945

a number of potential meeting points, such as the central lounge pit, with its long, low-slung bench that invites weary passengers to rest. The cafeteria's mezzanine-level seating area was meant to provide a privileged view of the main check-in space below. Small details, such as the embracing curves of the passageways or the convenient placement of the easy-to-grip handrails, added welcoming touches. From a farewell conversation to an information-gathering mission, the varied spaces of the terminal were designed to promote clustering.

EZRA STILES AND MORSE COLLEGES
YALE UNIVERSITY
NEW HAVEN, CONNECTICUT
1958–62

It was the Stiles and Morse colleges at Yale University that best reflected Saarinen's approach to inhabitation and clustering. In 1955 Yale had purchased land with the intention of building two new structures for student housing, either dormitories or colleges. Yale president A. Whitney Griswold had the vision for the project, and in 1958, Old Dominion Foundation chairman Paul Mellon donated $15 million—half of which was intended for construction and professional fees for the buildings—to make it a reality. By April 1958 Saarinen was making site and design studies, although he did not yet have the commission. As one of the university's planners and the architect of its recently completed and highly acclaimed David S. Ingalls Hockey Rink, he was confident that the project would be his. In fact, there was considerable reluctance to awarding Saarinen the commission due to the inaccuracy of his estimates (particularly regarding costs) for the hockey rink. Nevertheless, by the following April he had finally been selected.[7]

If Saarinen's concern was keeping to the $6.2 million budget, President Griswold's was the question of colleges versus dorms. In his "Proposal for Strengthening the Residential College System in Yale University," issued in April 1958, Griswold justified the need for both buildings to be colleges. He pointed out, inaccurately, that there were only four universities with the college system: Oxford and Cambridge in England, and Harvard and Yale in the United States. Much more than merely housing, the college provided an academic way of life, with meal service, cultural activities, sport, student study, and seminars with the "college master" all taking place in one location for a relatively small population. It was, according to Griswold, a microcosm of social life and the basis of the Yale education system.[8]

The proposal clearly made an impact. Shortly after its publication, the university's trustees decided that the two structures would be colleges. Each would have a capacity of 250 students and the total gross area would be approximately 237,600 square feet. One would be dedicated to Ezra Stiles, who graduated from Yale and served as its president from 1778 to 1795, the other to another Yale alumnus, Samuel F. B. Morse, who invented the telegraph in 1832. The site chosen for the colleges was located between Broadway to the west, Tower Parkway to the north and east, and York Street to the south.

The definition of college and context were major concerns for Eero Saarinen when outlining the project. Saarinen endorsed Griswold's preference for colleges and proposed to make collegiate community life a central aspect of his design. As he saw it, the challenge would be to transmit through architecture "the spirit and meaning" of college life. In November 1959, Saarinen wrote in the project statement for the colleges: "Somehow the architecture had to make clear this was not a group of dormitories, but *colleges*. The more we studied and thought about their function and purpose, the more

LEFT Ezra Stiles and Morse colleges, Yale University, New Haven, CT, 1958–62. Master plan
FOLLOWING SPREAD Ezra Stiles and Morse colleges, Yale University. Ezra Stoller © Esto

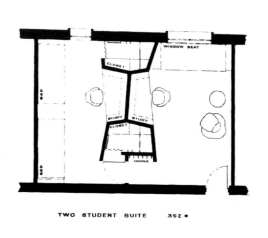

TWO STUDENT SUITE   352 ❖

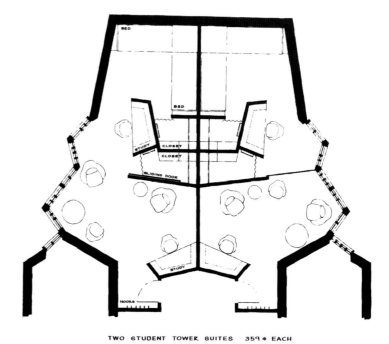

TWO STUDENT TOWER SUITES   359 ❖ EACH

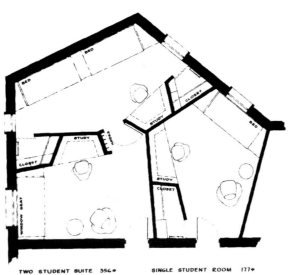

TWO STUDENT SUITE   356 ❖   SINGLE STUDENT ROOM   177 ❖

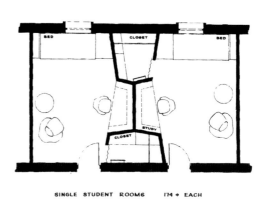

SINGLE STUDENT ROOMS   174 ❖ EACH

PREVIOUS SPREAD Ezra Stiles and Morse colleges, Yale University, New Haven, CT, 1958–62

ABOVE Ezra Stiles and Morse colleges, Yale University. Plan of dormitory rooms

convinced we became that the emphasis of these colleges must be on the individual."[9] That individual, he subsequently specified, was not an anonymous integer in a group, but a particular, individualized person.

Systematic interviews with students at Yale and other universities led to this conviction. "Talks with students strengthened our belief that rooms should be as individual as possible, as random as those in an old inn rather than as standardized as those in a modern motel," said Saarinen, who had been familiar with the Yale environment since his student days. Diversity—"many different rooms, rooms in towers, rooms of varying shapes and sizes and kinds and window and study arrangements"—would thus be the key to ensuring an individualized college experience. In the final design, the rooms were personalized in terms of their locations, their particular views, their sizes, and their shapes—72 percent of the rooms are singles, something the student residents still appreciate today.[10]

For Saarinen diversity was more than just the antithesis of repetition—it represented an antidote to modernism's unit-based anonymity. Having built the General Motors Technical Center in Warren, Michigan (1947–56), along modernist lines, he knew that its current vocabulary could result in a limitless sameness unbefitting the diversity he sought. "Flatness, lightness, glistening aluminum and glass, smoothness instead of rough texture and the play of light and shade—all these," he argued in the project statement, "could neither express the spirit we wanted nor be compatible with our neighboring buildings." Thus, at Yale Saarinen avoided the right angle altogether, and laid out the buildings in a clustered manner with a variety of spatial configurations.

An organic scheme is evident in the disposition of the colleges, which are united by the functional and economical necessity of grouping common spaces, such as kitchens and service areas. The variously shaped rooms were organized around stairwells and toilets, mainly in groupings of five, and were accessible from courts. Although they obviously refer to a functional model, each of these circulation-service-room clusters acquires a varied form due to the diversity of its constituent parts; just as most of the rooms were uniquely shaped, so were the small, citadel-like clusters they formed. Thus, Saarinen established a geometric pattern that organized the college plans like a live form, stressing the idea of diversity within a unitary whole. By all accounts, he was obsessed with proportion and geometry, and his use of polygonal clusters owes something to the fractal geometry popularized by mathematician Benoît Mandelbrot.

In addition to being a nontraditional way of arranging space, the cluster contrasts with the medieval cloister, which implies a building type. Thus, in the colleges, cloister and cluster relate to preconceived forms and to ways of gathering, fixed patterns and free solutions, tradition and novelty. When Saarinen began considering how to design

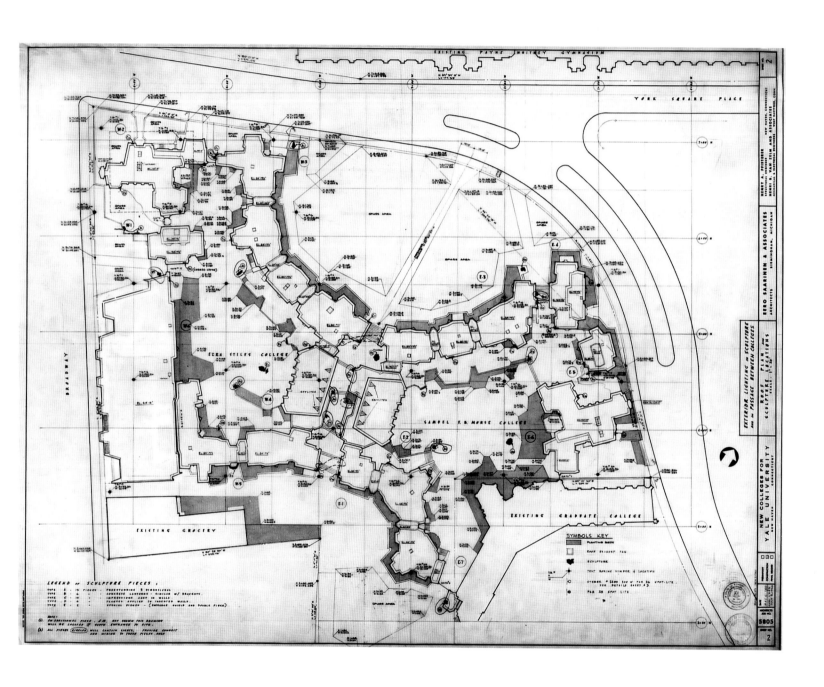

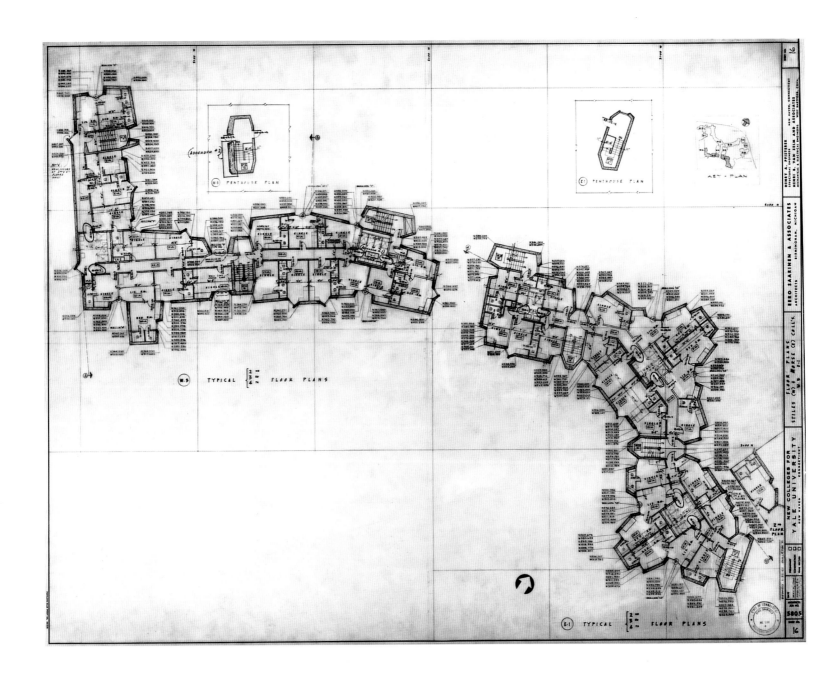

the Yale colleges he conducted his research in a way in which it is possible to detect these two divergent ideas. On the one hand, he collected data from other significant buildings—a process involving typological studies. On the other, he investigated ways of recreating, in a contemporary vein, the way of life in traditional monasteries.

The siting of the colleges was also considered contextually. In some early 1959 schemes the proposal is related, in a semicircular form, to the neighboring neo-Gothic Payne Whitney Gymnasium designed by John Russell Pope in 1932. The semi-circular form reflected the studies made by the New Haven Planning Commission for a road to the north and east of the gymnasium that would eliminate traffic on Tower Parkway. Saarinen also took particular interest in the way some of the other colleges, such Trumbull and Bradford, approximated medieval cloisters with their sequential courtyards. His project statement specifically mentions the use and configuration of courts at Yale. He appreciated the way they created specific perspectives, connected people and place, and infused the structure with the soothing, syncopated rhythm of open and enclosed spaces to offset the frenzy of contemporary life.

In Saarinen's colleges, the clustering concept worked on three levels. The initial cluster was based on the rooms and their attendant service and circulation areas. The secondary cluster involved courts, which, in turn, comprised multiple room-service-circulation clusters and were scattered around the two colleges. And the third was understood to be the colleges themselves as a kind of distinctive cluster within the context of the campus as a whole. One source of inspiration for the neo-medieval form of the multilevel structures, which involved stepped passageways, winding alleys, and little "monastic" dormitory rooms, was the eleventh-century towers of San Gimignano, Italy.

Nevertheless, Saarinen had no intention of making a literal translation of Gothic forms. He sought the translation of the monastic-inspired college life into the diversity implied by contemporary life. "Each age must create its own architecture out of its own technology, and one which is expressive of its own Zeitgeist—the spirit of the time," he said at the 1954 AIA convention. Thus, unlike Yale's 1917 Harkness Memorial tower, which architect James Gamble Rogers based directly on Rouen's Butter Tower, or Pope's Payne Whitney Gymnasium, which was partially inspired by Liverpool Cathedral, Saarinen's colleges were contemporary in style and relationship to their context. Saarinen's architecture can thus be seen to be operating dialectically between the spirit of place and the spirit of time. Representing an alternative to mainstream modernism, Saarinen's work balances context and Zeitgeist.[11]

To further distinguish the buildings in their context, he intentionally set them off from their surrounding structures with a rough-hewn exterior stone finish that was completely different from the smooth sandstone or tidy brickwork of the other Yale buildings. For Saarinen, the question was how to make a contemporary stone wall that would subtly evoke the medieval without reverting to old-fashioned techniques. His solution featured reinforced concrete with inlaid crushed stone. The highly textured surface was, according to Saarinen, an attempt to reproduce the effect of "the walls of old Pennsylvania houses, where worn plaster reveals the stonework, or the stone walls of the Cotswold in England."

Another way he distinguished the colleges was by installing a series of abstract sculptures around them. As one approaches the buildings, the array of sculptures come into focus. Designed by sculptor Costantino Nivola, the forty-six pieces—made using a mortar similar to the one used on the college walls—vary from freestanding three-dimensional works to impressions cast into the walls themselves. Saarinen must have conceived of these various sculptural groups as a way of directing the attention of the visitor. He made careful studies of their placement so that they would be well integrated with the buildings. His vision was perhaps that each piece would be discovered individually and that the discovery of one would lead to the discovery of the next one beyond it. Their position in relation to each other and to the buildings creates a dynamic sense of progress and draws attention to different aspects of the buildings' forms.[12] The result enhances the concept of formal diversity that Saarinen sought with the buildings, and follows the model for life in the colleges.

FOLLOWING SPREAD Ezra Stiles and Morse colleges, Yale University, New Haven, CT, 1958–62
Ezra Stoller © Esto

Following his father's interest in comprehensive design, Saarinen envisioned design in a broad scope, from planning to architecture to furniture design: "I believe very strongly that the whole field of design is all one thing. Therefore my interest in furniture,"[13] he told a friend in 1948. Chairs and tables, the basic elements of any interior environment, offered themselves up to him as a means for further experimentation with ways of redesigning contemporary life.

The Organic Design in Home Furnishings collection, made for the Museum of Modern Art's 1940–41 international furniture competition, marked Saarinen's debut as a furniture designer. Organized by MoMA director Eliot F. Noyes together with Ira Hirshman, the competition was judged by a panel that included Alvar Aalto, Marcel Breuer, Alfred Barr, Edward Durell Stone, and Frank Parrish. Saarinen and Charles Eames submitted a joint entry and won in two different categories: seating for a living room and other furniture for a living room (the other categories included lighting fixtures and outdoor furniture). Their entries included a side chair, a conversation chair, a relaxation chair, a lounge, a sofa unit, a dining table, a coffee table, and modular cases. The different pieces were designed to be fabricated in wood or plywood shell, and finished with either upholstery, fabric, rubber, or a veneer of Honduras mahogany. In spite of the prizes and the collaboration with the Haskelite Manufacturing Corporation and the Heywood-Wakefield Company, the Organic Design collection was never mass-produced.[14]

It is relevant, however, in terms of Saarinen's body of work not only because it was a precursor to many of his later furniture designs, but also because of its systemic organization. The Organic Design collection was, first and foremost, a series. Each piece was designed on an eighteen-inch module; bases of differing lengths were used to combine two, three, or more units. The integral design approach endowed each piece with a distinct identity while ensuring its harmonic convergence with all the other pieces in the group. As such, it reflected a crucial concept Saarinen had absorbed from his father:

> Perhaps the most important thing I learned from my father was that in any design problem one should seek the solution in terms of the next largest thing. If the problem is an ashtray, then the way it relates to the table will influence its design. If the problem is a chair, then its solution must be found in the way it relates to the room cube. If it is a building, the townscape will affect the solution.[15]

It's no wonder, then, that the illustration Saarinen and Eames presented with their collection showed three of the pieces—the side chair, the conversation chair, and the modular cases—in the context of an actual room.

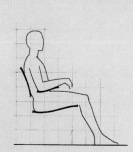

CONVERSATION

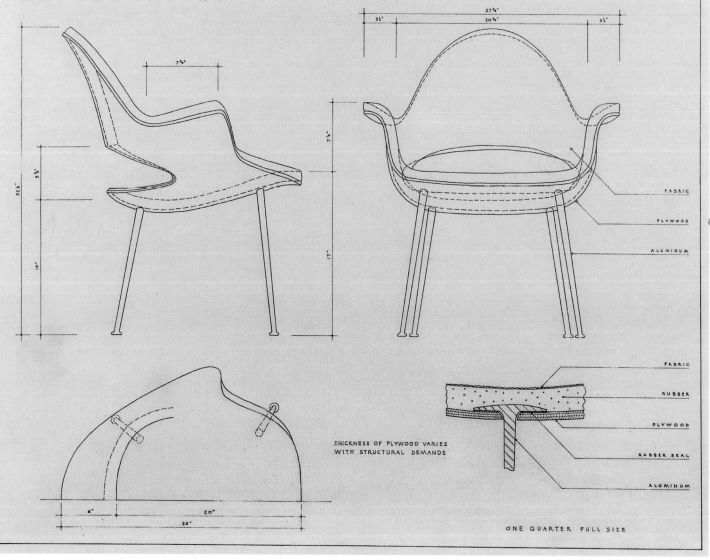

FABRIC

PLYWOOD

ALUMINUM

FABRIC

RUBBER

PLYWOOD

RUBBER SEAL

ALUMINUM

THICKNESS OF PLYWOOD VARIES
WITH STRUCTURAL DEMANDS

ONE QUARTER FULL SIZE

LOUNGING SHAPE

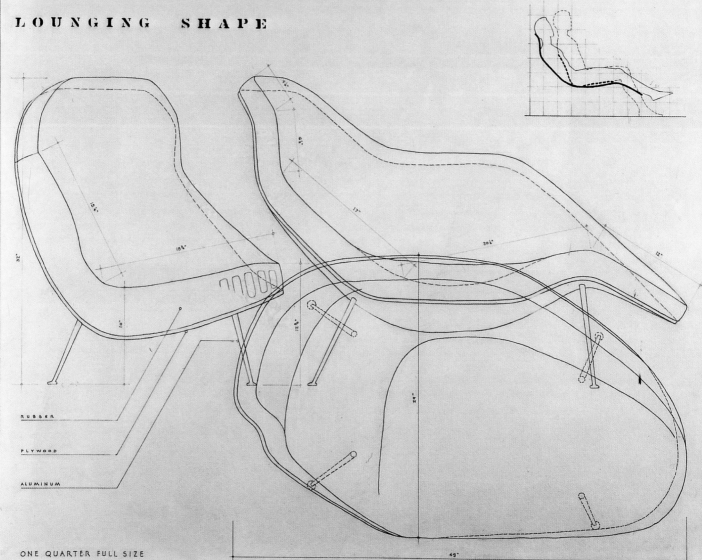

RUBBER

PLYWOOD

ALUMINUM

ONE QUARTER FULL SIZE

The Organic Design collection collaboration was important for both Saarinen and Eames in their respective pursuits of furniture design. This collaboration meant the association of two very similar ways of working in architecture and design—for Saarinen, design was based on procedures, and for Eames, design was a "method of action." As Eames's associate Don Albison pointed out, the living room seating series shows Saarinen's influence, whereas one detects Charles Eames's input in the modular pieces. Both Saarinen and Eames developed subsequent designs based on molding plywood into compound curvatures, one of the two new manufacturing techniques they devised for the Organic Design series (the other being a type of welding, invented by Chrysler, that made it possible to join rubber and wood). But of the two, it was Eames whose work would become most closely associated with the modular furniture featured in the collection. Charles Eames based many of his later designs on the Organic Design chairs. According to design historian Pat Kirkham, the list of Eames chairs that were based directly on pieces from the Organic Design series includes: the plastic shell, 1950; the wire shell, 1952; the La Fonda chair, 1961; the Soft Pad chair, 1969; and the Aluminum Group, 1958.[16]

The Womb Chair, Saarinen's enveloping, softly angled, upholstered lounger, suggests that his conception of inhabiting most definitely involved comfort. Designed between 1946 and 1948, shortly after he joined Knoll Associates in 1943 and designed the No. 61 lounge chair, the Womb Chair—the No. 70 lounge chair—was cozy, irregular, and soft. In a word, it was comforting. It even came with an optional footrest or ottoman. The very notion of comfort had essentially been absent from the discourse of the avant-garde for some time. They preferred functionalist criteria when considering housing and furniture. But for Saarinen those criteria left a lot to be desired. "I designed the Womb Chair because there seemed to be a need for a large and really comfortable chair to take the place of the old overstuffed chair. These dreadnoughts disappeared from modern interiors. . . . But the need for such chairs has not passed. Today, more than ever before, we need to relax." While his statement clearly favors the comfort so disdained by modernism, it also vividly reflects his own prioritization of human impulse. Undoubtedly, Saarinen was attuned to contemporary culture's increasingly psychological orientation. As he says, comparing his early model for Knoll and the Womb Chair: "The Womb Chair also attempts to achieve a psychological comfort by providing a big cuplike shell into which you can curl up and pull up your legs." Saarinen had himself photographed sitting informally on the Womb Chair, his calm expression proving that people really do feel less insecure in the womb, a point that he elucidated in a 1949 letter to his client J. Irwin

Miller: "I am glad to hear that you like the big chair. You might be interested to know that its unofficial name is the 'Womb Chair,' because it was designed on the theory that a great number of people have never felt really comfortable and secure since they left the womb. The chair is an attempt to rectify this maladjustment in our civilization."[17]

Saarinen stressed that the form of the Womb Chair was a consequence of new ways of seating: "People sit differently today than in the Victorian era," he observed. "They want to sit lower and they like to slouch." But that didn't mean that they should be without support: "In my first postwar chair, I attempted to shape the slouch in an organized way by giving support for the back as well as the seat, shoulders, and head. The Womb Chair also has three planes of support."[18] Such considerations regarding the shape are evident in the chair's United States Patent Office file, dated 13 February 1951. In the patent statement, Saarinen explains the importance of the form's curves, and how they allow for the possibility of upholstering without the use of gussets. And in the corresponding diagrams, he shows how the surfaces providing three planes of support are derived from a cone. Produced by Knoll Associates beginning in 1948, the Womb was the first fiberglass chair to be mass-produced in America.[19]

In his Pedestal series, a bold collection of single-legged tables and chairs, designed from 1955 to 1957 and also produced by Knoll, Saarinen explored the relationship between innovation and inhabitation. According to his 1958 statement on the Pedestal furniture, the revolutionary design was motivated principally by a unitary aesthetic concern:

> The undercarriage of chairs and tables in a typical interior makes an ugly, confusing, unrestful world. I wanted to clear up the slum of legs. I wanted to make the chair all one thing again. All the great furniture of the past, from Tutankhamun's chair to Thomas Chippendale's, have always been a structural total. With our excitement over plastic and plywood shells, we grew away from this structural total. As now manufactured, the pedestal furniture is half-plastic, half-metal. I look forward to the day when the plastic industry has advanced to the point where the chair will be one material, as designed.[20]

Several pencil sketches, in which Saarinen first articulated his ideas for the series, show that the idea of unity was fundamental. As detailed technical drawings for construction indicate, the streamlined silhouette masked a rather complex structure. In fact, the design involved two principal substructures: a reinforced fiberglass shell, which was meant to accommodate the foam-rubber cushion and seat rests; and a cast-aluminum pedestal, which was joined to the shell by means of a rod. This complex

ABOVE AND RIGHT Tulip Chair, Knoll Associates, 1956. Advertisement

KNOLL ASSOCIATES, INC. FURNITURE AND TEXTILES 575 MADISON AVENUE. NEW YORK 22

system was hidden beneath the serene uniformity of the curving shape; in short, structure was subordinated to form. Knoll literature details the mass-produced elements of the Pedestal series. The Tulip arm and side chairs were available in white, gray, or charcoal. And the iconic, one-leg tables could be ordered in different sizes as a side table, coffee table, dining table, or conference table, in a choice of white marble, walnut veneer, or white plastic laminate.[21]

The Pedestal chair was clearly related to Charles Eames's plastic side chair (1950–53), in particular the shape of its seat and back. But evidence suggests that Saarinen's design was inspired by the study of a wide array of contemporary chairs. A drawing made in his office shows the Pedestal chair compared in profile to a 1952 wire upholstered chair by Harry Bertoia, the 1951 Margherita chair by Franco Albini, a similar chair by Kurt Nordstrom, the Organic Design side chair, and the aforementioned Eames side chair.[22]

Saarinen perceived contemporary interiors as necessarily impersonal and, at the same time, possessed of an individual identity linked to their inhabitants. For Saarinen, mass-produced furniture actually constituted the structure of the interior environment. Personal identity was to be provided by ornamental or nonstructural elements, such as art, books, flowers, and the miscellaneous trappings of life.[23] Saarinen's interiors, such as a dining room with Pedestal series furniture, reflect this conception: Maintaining an impersonal substratum—which Saarinen himself defined as classical—they retain a personal identity.

In the Organic Design, Womb Chair, and Pedestal series, Saarinen's process pushed the field of furniture design to its limits. By looking closely at the way people actually sit—or slump—he forged new forms and structures that, in his search for meaning, reflected a comprehensive modern attitude toward design, an attitude that enhanced human experience and the new challenges involved in contemporary life.

BUILDING

The awareness of the thinking and technology
of our time is for me an ever-present challenge.

The Latin word *aedificare* refers to the making of a shelter. More than simply building, the assembly of parts and materials, *aedificare* describes an activity primarily concerned with inhabitation.[1] This age-old distinction between building as *aedificare* and building as construction is the basis, following the latter's more scientific bias, of the enduring split between architecture and engineering—a split that has kept the visionaries or design innovators on one side of any given project and the technicians or structural innovators on another.

Eero Saarinen was one of the very few architects who could convincingly bridge the gap. In his practice, *Kunstform,* the form linked to the artistic, and *Werkform*, the form strictly necessary for support, were not divorced. Unlike most twentieth-century de signers, his technical achievements were not only as remarkable as his stylistic ones, they were as remarkable as any made by the leading engineers of his day. Saarinen pioneered structures that combined functional design, construction, mechanical services, and habitability.[2]

Two of his most famous buildings, Dulles International Airport outside Washington, DC, and the Jefferson National Expansion Memorial in St. Louis—better known as the Gateway Arch—provide rich examples of his astonishing ability to function as both designing architect and technical engineer. Innovative yet graceful, they reveal his integral approach to the structural, constructive, and functional problems of contemporary design.

Both projects show how this integral approach to technical problems transcends the resolution of the merely practical. Behind them we can see a comprehensive understanding of technique, in which there is no schism between artistic and technical creativity. Both Dulles Airport and the Gateway Arch reflect Saarinen's remarkable resolution of practical issues and projection of symbolic form and monumentality in the cultural arena.

DULLES INTERNATIONAL AIRPORT
CHANTILLY, VIRGINIA
1958–62

In 1958, when Saarinen accepted the commission from the Federal Aviation Administration (FAA) to design an airport outside of Washington, DC, his TWA Terminal was well under way. And while he was certainly able to draw on his experience designing for Idlewild, the new airport was an entirely different proposition. Named for John Foster Dulles, who had served as secretary of state in the Eisenhower administration, and located on a 9,800-acre site in Chantilly, Virginia, 27 miles from the federal capital, Dulles cost $175 million and was the largest airport in the United States at the time it was designed. More important, it was the first commercial airport to be designed specifically for jets.[3]

Saarinen considered the jet factor to be an entirely new functional problem—one he would have to solve through design ingenuity. But he approached the project by systematically collecting data at various airports, just as he had for the TWA Terminal. "We sent out teams with counters and stop-watches to see what people really do at airports, how far they walk, their interchange problems. We analyzed special problems of jets, examined schedules, peak loads, effects of weather. We studied baggage handling, economics, methods of operations; and so on." The amassed information was translated into a series of about forty charts that showed detailed comparisons of time, distance, and locale. One graphed the walking distance from parked car to plane at airports in Dallas, Detroit, Philadelphia, St. Louis, Washington, Chicago, and Los Angeles in comparison to the much shorter distance Saarinen was proposing for Dulles.[4]

Saarinen's methodology—his zealous gathering, analysis, and charting of airport information in order to establish a model for the building's functionality—was strongly influenced not only by his father, who had made a thorough functional analysis for the construction of the Helsinki Railway Station (1904–14), but also by industrial designer Norman Bel Geddes. Bel Geddes' futuristic buildings—such as his General Motors Pavilion for the 1939–40 New York World's Fair—made him a model for young American architects, and Saarinen was no exception. In the spring of 1938, after he had finished his European study trip and before beginning teaching at Cranbrook, Saarinen spent a short period of time working for Bel Geddes in New York. There he was able to practice his father's way of addressing problems systematically, rather than just conceptually, by using quantifiable data and functionality studies. His fact-finding missions for both TWA and Dulles clearly correlate to the methods Bel Geddes employed in his own proposals. In *Horizons*, his 1932 book about design for the future, Bel Geddes included a detailed functional study of a terminal designed for St. Louis's Lambert Airport. He also documented passenger and plane traffic on the airport's different levels, as well as the terminal's illumination, services, and points of access.[5] Bel Geddes addressed the question of the airport systematically, introducing such innovative con-

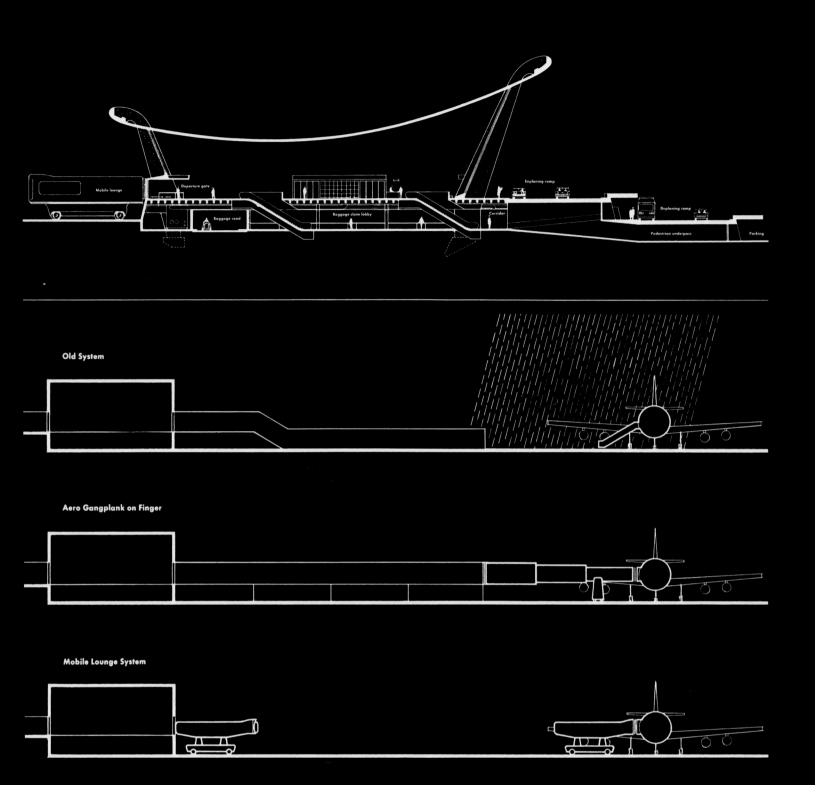

Old System

Aero Gangplank on Finger

Mobile Lounge System

ABOVE Dulles Airport Terminal, Chantilly, VA, 1958–62
Section drawings and mobile lounge schematics
RIGHT Chrysler Mobile Lounge, Dulles International Airport
President John F. Kennedy exiting a mobile lounge

cepts as a rotary airport for New York harbor. But it was not only his methodical way of working that must have impressed Saarinen. His streamlined forms can also be seen as a precedent for those Saarinen used to define TWA and Dulles.

According to Saarinen, analysis of the collected data indicated three critical issues for the Dulles design team: the time and inconvenience of getting passengers to and from planes; the heavy cost of taxiing jet planes; and the increasing need for flexibility in the operations and servicing of aircraft.[6] With these considerations in mind, Saarinen hired a number of consultants, including structural and mechanical engineers from the firms of Ammann & Whitney and Burns & McDowell, and airport expert Charles Landrum. Together they considered various ways of providing better access to the aircraft for both the passengers and the service personnel.

They reasoned that the problem could be solved most efficiently "by combining the departure lounge and the moving vehicle into a single convenience, and by combining *that* with a covered gangplank that hitches directly to the plane."[7] This was one of the first uses of the revolutionary system of mobile lounges, also employed in Europe. These roving, room-sized people movers would ferry large groups from the gate to the plane, thereby reducing the distance individuals had to traverse between check-in and boarding. Convenient and comfortable for passengers, the mobile units also provided added flexibility for aircraft service.

Convincing FAA and Dulles officials of the mobile lounge plan's efficacy and feasibility was, however, a considerable challenge. Incorporating the units meant not only a significant change in procedure and equipment for every airline operating at Dulles, but a radical reconfiguration of what an airport could be. Of course, there was some resistance. So Saarinen turned to Charles Eames, who produced an animated color film, *The Expanding Airport,* that explained, through drawings and diagrams, the advantages for both passengers and airlines of the mobile lounge proposal.[8] Armed with Eames's visual aid, Saarinen's presentation came to life and his mobile lounge proposal prevailed.

As developed by the Chrysler Corporation, each unit could accommodate up to eighty passengers, effectively serving the same function as the conventional buses being used in some European airports, such as London, Paris, Amsterdam, and Frankfurt.[9] But because it was designed with a vertical adjustment mechanism to seamlessly connect to both the terminal gate and the plane's access door, it eliminated the time-consuming upstairs-downstairs routine of moving passengers from the departure level down to a tarmac-level bus and then back up to board the plane. Not incidentally, it also protected them from exposure to the elements.

What was truly ingenious about Saarinen's mobile lounge plan was the way it became the basis not only for the functional scheme Saarinen developed for the whole of the Dulles Terminal, but also for the stylistic concept he created for the building, both inside and out. Conscious of Dulles's dual status as the international gateway to the country's capital city, and the world's first airport to be built specifically for jet travel, Saarinen envisioned a monumental structure that would appear to rise up out of the surrounding airfields like "something between earth and sky." His sloping lines and thrusting angles were thus a means of conveying a sense of movement and the exciting adventure of jet travel, and simultaneously a way of offsetting the static architecture generally associated with monuments. As he stated, "We exaggerated and dramatized the outward slope as well as the wide compressive flange at the rear of the columns to give the colonnade a dynamic and soaring look as well as a stately and dignified one."[10]

Sketches of his first attempts at the terminal's resolution point to various formal and structural options.[11] One design constraint was the need for a canopy to shelter passengers arriving by car. Initial studies show proposals in which the canopy is incorporated into the roofline in a manner that hints at the bays of the final structural system. Other early sketches demonstrate attempts to find a solution involving cables bolstered by two sets of supports, although they reveal Saarinen's doubts about how to design the supports to ensure stability. The drawings that point toward the definitive solution involve an arched structure reminiscent of Saarinen's earlier proposal for the Ingalls Hockey Rink at Yale University. With light suspension-bridge cables stretched in a catenary curve and concrete piers sloping outward to counteract the pull of the cables, the final Dulles Terminal proposal was, according to Saarinen, "like a huge, continuous hammock suspended between concrete trees." To other observers the form resembled Bedouin tents, or *jaimas*. In fact, Saarinen had already devised a similar cable-based tensile structure for his 1949 Aspen Music Tent. But, perhaps more than his own previous projects, Saarinen's design for Dulles was influenced by a number of buildings designed by his contemporaries.[12]

Among the principal precedents for Saarinen's structural schema was the Dorton Arena in Raleigh, North Carolina. Conceived by Matthew Nowicki, who had worked in Saarinen's office, the arena was built between 1948 and 1953. Its suspension-cable structure demonstrated Nowicki's pioneering use of what is known as the "director's chair" principle: a pair of inclined reinforced-concrete arches supporting a system of tension cables to form a sturdy saddle-shaped surface. Previous suspension cable structures had been plagued by the problem of flutter. But Nowicki's design—which was

FOLLOWING SPREAD Dulles Airport Terminal, Chantilly, VA, 1958–62
Ezra Stoller © Esto

developed by architect W. H. Dietrick and engineers from Severud-Elstad-Krueger after the architect's untimely death in 1950—resolved that issue by using two sets of orthogonal cables.[13]

Another arena, the experimental Hipódromo de la Zarzuela in Madrid, Spain, was similarly influential. Engineered in 1936 by Eduardo Torroja, with architects C. Arniches and M. Domínguez, the building featured an innovative use of materials and forms that exemplified 1950s structural expressionism. Evidently, the Spanish stadium had become legendary in the United States, as Saarinen felt compelled to make a pilgrimage there just before beginning work on Dulles. It's no wonder, then, that his initial sketches for the terminal bear a certain resemblance to the Hipódromo's concrete-membrane cantilevers. But, in a broader sense, Dulles responded to the climate generated by the decade's many prominent structural expressionists. Félix Candela, for example, used concrete shells in his 1956 San Antonio de las Huertas church in Mexico City. In Italy, Pier Luigi Nervi and Riccardo Morandi also were experimenting with daring forms in concrete during this period.[14]

Dulles officially opened on 19 November 1962. Its final design, which retained the apparent simplicity of Saarinen's earliest sketches, belied its elaborate structural complexities. Having resolved the traffic problem through the introduction of mobile lounges, he laid out a linear, two-level plan in which the distance between entry door and loading platform was a mere 150 feet. The logical placement of ticketing, check-in, and boarding gates on the upper floor, which arriving passengers accessed via an enplaning ramp, and the baggage claim, hotel accommodation booths, and rental car services on the lower floor, provided for a smooth flow throughout the terminal. In coordination with the terminal's structural system, which Saarinen based on 40-by-150-foot bays, the mobile units were built so that two could fit into each bay. Originally, twenty-four mobile lounge positions were planned, anticipating extensions that would be in keeping with the original design.[15]

On both its front and rear facades, the 150-by-600-foot main concourse, which has demonstrated its flexibility in a recent extension, was endowed with a row of angular concrete columns. Situated at 40-foot intervals and measuring 65 and 40 feet high, respectively, the jutting columns were designed to support pairs of light suspension-bridge cables which, in turn, were needed to support the roof's curved concrete panels. Each of these elements, the columns, the cables, and the curved roofline, was important functionally as well as stylistically. The columns, in addition to their obvious structural function, were purposely designed with scarped bases and vertical tapering to exaggerate their bearing quality and the monumentality of the entire airport. The catenary roof form not only added to the building's dynamic exterior, but its convex surface also improved acoustic quality inside the building by dispersing sound—a valuable feature in the busy shuffle of an international terminal. And the suspension cables' amazing combination of light weight, strength, and flexibility—which enabled Saarinen to achieve the pristine inverted arc of the roof—formed stiffer supports once the poured concrete and roof panels had set. The terminal was therefore able to avoid certain wind-load effects, such as fluttering, that threatened the stability of other cable-based structures.

In each design choice Saarinen made for Dulles, it is possible to see not only the solution to a structural requirement and the expression of a formal goal, but also the awareness of the way aesthetics can assimilate the human body with an architectural object. As critic Allan Temko stated:

> Every detail—doors, canopies, balustrades—is scaled for humans, as in a Gothic cathedral, so that the impression of size is continually reinforced between them and the grand elements of the composition: the low entrance between two columns, for example, is a measure of their grandeur. But more than this, the entire design is based on recognition of the functional as well as the emotional needs of man: this is one large airport—the terminal at Brasilia is perhaps the only other—where the traveler is humanly considered from his arrival to departure.[16]

Dulles thus achieved monumentality by combining functional flexibility, structural requirement, and formal expression. Saarinen could not conceal his satisfaction with the design, claiming, "I think this airport is the best thing I have done. It is going to be really good. Maybe it will even explain what I believe about architecture."[17]

PREVIOUS SPREAD Dulles International Airport Terminal Building, Chantilly, VA, 1958–62
Ezra Stoller © Esto

JEFFERSON NATIONAL EXPANSION MEMORIAL
ST. LOUIS, MISSSOURI
1947–65

Ten years before anyone had contemplated a Dulles Terminal, let alone an international jetport, Saarinen had already designed and redesigned the Jefferson National Expansion Memorial, St. Louis's riverside monument better known as the Gateway Arch.

First proposed by Luther Ely Smith, the St. Louis monument was proposed as a way to commemorate president Thomas Jefferson, the Louisiana Purchase, and the opening of the trans-Mississippi West. By 1933 Smith had established the Jefferson National Expansion Memorial Association, the governing body that would oversee the politically fraught, decades-long process of erecting a fitting tribute to one of America's most influential leaders and the westward expansion he envisioned. Two years later, in 1935, thanks to the steady pressure of Smith's association, President Franklin D. Roosevelt issued an executive order for $30 million to establish the Jefferson National Expansion Memorial (JNEM) as a national monument. From that point it took two more years before the promised $9 million land grant was actually provided, more than ten until a national architectural competition for its development was announced, and another thirty before the project was considered complete.

The selected site for the memorial—an 82.5-acre plot of riverfront running from the east bank of the Mississippi all the way to Fourth Street in downtown St. Louis—was equivalent to forty city blocks. From its inception, the project was subject to continuous alterations. One early plan proposed a group of seven buildings and statues, the grandest of which would be dedicated to Jefferson and the Louisiana Purchase. Another called for one large statue of Jefferson by the river, three museums, and several tall obelisks. A third reduced the number of buildings to two.[18]

In 1947, with a mounting number of proposals but still no clear plan, the association announced a national architectural competition. Its rather far-ranging guidelines for developing the site required designs for one or more architectural monuments, an open-air theater, recreational facilities, a parking lot, a heliport, and the relocation of not only railroad tracks but also a substantial part of the interstate highway.[19] Additionally, designers were advised that their entries should emphasize landscaping and make provisions for the possible inclusion of a few small-scale reproductions of typical St. Louis buildings, one or more museums, and a living memorial to Jefferson.

With these constraints in mind, Saarinen entered the competition. He was one of five architects selected to enter the second phase. Among the 172 first-round entries, Saarinen beat out one by his father, Eliel Saarinen. Eero Saarinen's plan, perhaps the most ambitious of the five semifinalists, was the result of a team effort that involved design architect J. Henderson Barr, landscape architect Dan Kiley, graphic designer Alexander H. Girard, and sculptor Lily Swann, then Saarinen's wife. It included a large

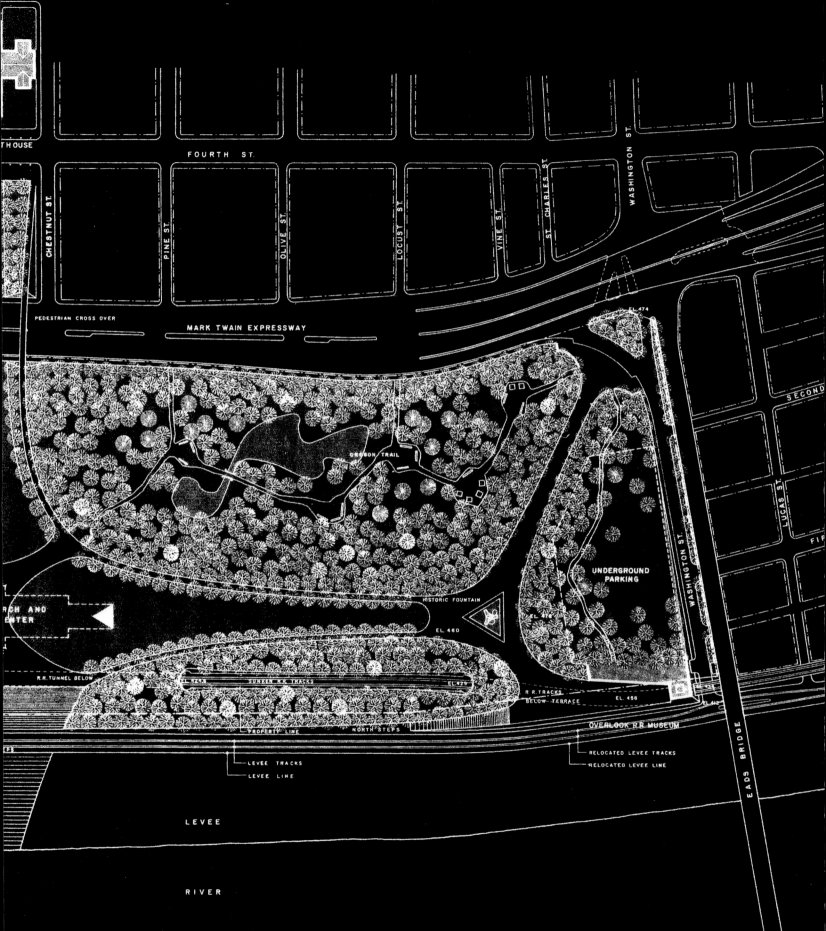

memorial arch on the riverbank opposite the Old Courthouse building and a series of commercial buildings, such as banks and hotels with corresponding parking, along the stretch between Third and Fourth Streets. By the base of the arch, which spanned 630 feet and was rounded in the structurally optimized form of an inverted catenary, there was space for a long mall, alongside of which he projected a series of gardens and courtyards with sculptures and murals. While the arch was certainly the main feature of the proposal, the other structures revolved around another central element: a park. Amidst its trees, Saarinen set the Old Cathedral, the open-air theater, and a little village of early pioneer houses.[20]

Between the first and second competition phases there was a reduction in the program. The buildings between Third and Fourth streets were discarded, the heliport and underground parking scrapped, and the living memorial deemed extraneous. Saarinen revised his proposal accordingly, and with so much less building mass, the park became much more prominent. The arch, formerly set at 590 feet high, was rescaled to 630 feet, giving it a slightly more tapered or elongated profile. In his accompanying project statement Saarinen created a kind of narrative, explaining the reconfigured elements as a sequence of activities or experiences: Arriving by car. Entering through Washington Avenue to an observation plaza. Lunching at the riverside café. Attending a program at the open-air theater. Wandering around the village of pioneers. Promenading along the mall into the park. Touring the Old Courthouse or the Old Cathedral. Visiting the architectural and historic museums. Dining in the river restaurant. Exploring the historic arcade. And, finally, experiencing the view of it all from the top of the arch at nightfall.[21]

To the jury it sounded pretty good. Their decision to award Saarinen the $40,000 first prize was unanimous. Explanatory comments stressed how well the proposal satisfied the demands of the program, highlighting the ways it improved upon the first-phase proposal and its potential for exploiting the park. William W. Wurster and Richard J. Neutra, two of the more enthusiastic jurors, supported a statement saying that "the entire concept, full of exciting possibilities for actual achievement, is a work of a genius, and the memorial structure is of that high order which will rank it among the nation's greatest monuments."[22]

From the start, the development of the project was fraught with problems. Some were technical, such as the track relocation; others were financial. The railroad relocation issue was not resolved until 1957, and the budgetary difficulties lingered until 1960, the year construction began. In addition, despite the unanimous approval of Saarinen's revised plan, the association decided to further reduce its scope by eliminating the

ABOVE Gateway Arch, St. Louis, MO, 1948–64. Competition rendering
RIGHT Gateway Arch and State House

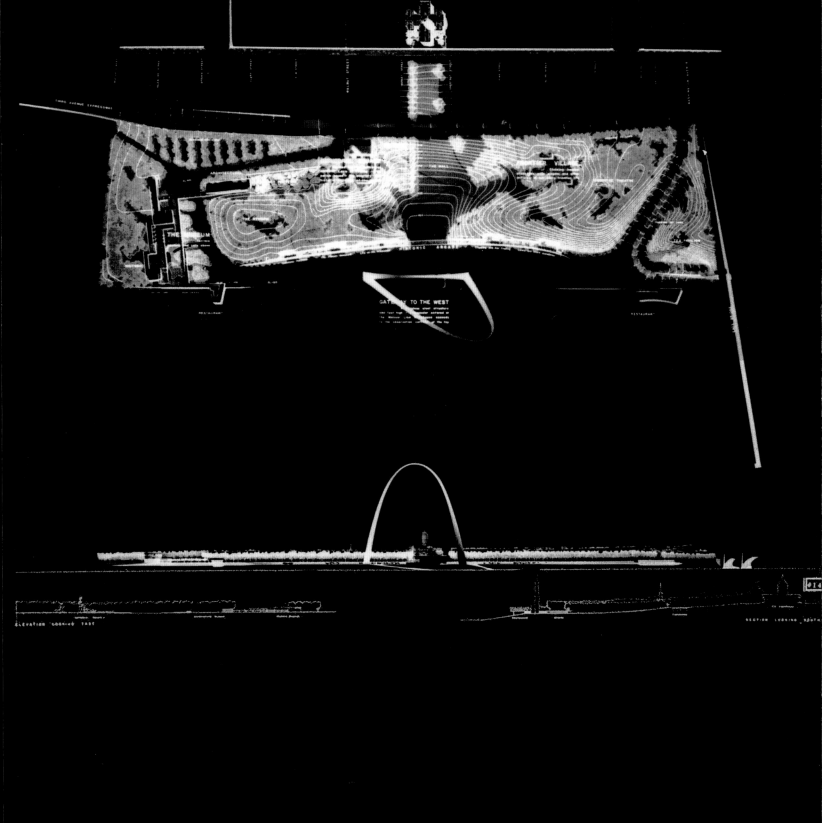

arcade, museums, village, restaurants, gardens, and theater. Then, just before construction was to begin, the National Park Service asked Saarinen to reinstate space for one museum. Thus, the final plan entailed only the arch, one museum—which Saarinen designed to be completely underground—and the surrounding park. The arch was completed on 28 October 1965. But the rest of the work continued until the museum opened in 1976.[23]

At the time of its construction, the Gateway Arch represented the greatest stressed-skin construction ever undertaken. Engineer Fred N. Severud, whom Saarinen had contracted to oversee the memorial's structural engineering, compared the structural behavior of the arch's triangular section to a blade of grass. His penchant for seeking inspiration in nature appealed to Saarinen, whose vision of the arch had, from its inception, been predicated on the kind of simple grace found in organic forms. Of course, Saarinen also understood that achieving such natural elegance in a man-made structure, especially one as massive as the arch, would require the kind of complex construction techniques Severud had mastered.[24]

And, indeed, it was complex. Based on the structural systems used for airplane wings or sailboat masts, the arch was built using a series of double-walled triangular pieces and arched section sides. The triangles were equilateral and measured 12 feet high per side. The arched sides ranged from 54 feet at the arch's base to 17 feet at its top. The skin, the thickness of which ran from three feet to a mere 7 and 5/8 inches, was comprised of a stainless steel outside layer that was 1/4 inch thick and a carbon-steel inner layer as thin as 3/8 inch. Up to the 300-foot level, the walls were filled with concrete reinforced by pre-stressed steel rods. Above that point, and up to the 630-foot peak, steel stiffeners were inserted between the iron walls instead of the concrete infill.[25]

This stressed skin technique had already been used in engineering. The Golden Gate Bridge towers (1933–37), for example, were devised from a similar cellular system.[26] And in building construction, R. Buckminster Fuller had proposed an aluminum stretched-skin surface for his Dymaxion House (1940–41). Saarinen himself had already toyed with the concept when he designed a metal shell for his Unfolding House in 1945. But its use on a scale as massive as the arch was completely unprecedented. Also unprecedented was the way it concealed the different internal construction systems: The welded-steel exterior plates masked the combination of concrete infill and cellular construction, giving the monument a totally unified appearance.

From the competition phase onwards, Saarinen spent as much energy working out the building process as the construction technique. Early sketches of the arch display

ABOVE Gateway Arch, St. Louis, MO, 1948–64
FOLLOWING SPREADS Gateway Arch. Working drawing and construction photos

various concepts, including the use of derricks that could climb up the arch's legs. The MacDonald Construction Company, the firm responsible for constructing the arch and the visitor center, did use derricks similar to the ones Saarinen sketched. For the first sections, the hoists were operated from the ground level. From the 72-foot level, a creeper derrick, or tilting platform, was used. At the 530-foot level a stabilizing strut was installed until the last of the 142 sections was put in place.[27]

The hollow interior of the arch—the vacuum of space between the three sides of the steel skeleton—was used to shelter a staircase and mechanical transportation system that would ferry visitors up to the arch's peak. Using a combination of Ferris wheel and elevator technology, two eight-capsule trams—one for each leg of the arch—ascended to the observation room on tracks by means of this internal funicular. Inside, each capsule was furnished with a cluster of five seats whose cylindrical forms combined aspects of Saarinen's Pedestal series and Womb Chair.

As he remarked in one of the project statements, Saarinen's primary concern in designing the memorial was "to create a monument that would have lasting significance and be a landmark of our time."[28] The curving arch, he believed, would express both timeless monumentality and contemporary dynamism by combining obvious references to classical arches with a sleek, aerodynamically curving form. His choice of stainless steel as the exterior material was intended to suggest permanence as well as progress. Yet for many of his contemporaries, Saarinen's choice of form and material symbolized less lofty ideals.

Just one week after Saarinen won the competition, Gilmore D. Clarke, a New York landscape architect and engineer, sent a letter to William W. Wurster, chairman of the JNEM competition jury, igniting a debate over the originality of Saarinen's proposal. Clark's letter pointed out the similarities between Saarinen's design, both in scale and appearance, to the arch designed by Adalberto Libera for the 1942 Roman Esposizione Universale. The Esposizione, a pet project of Benito Mussolini, was intended to celebrate Italian fascism, but never took place due to the outbreak of World War II. Clarke was actually less concerned by Saarinen's willingness to copy a design than by the particular design he chose to copy. "The pertinent question," Clarke wrote, "is not whether or not the design was plagiarized; rather it is whether or not, in the circumstances, it is appropriate to perpetuate the memory of Thomas Jefferson and to memorialize the Louisiana Purchase by constructing a monument similar in design to one originally created to glorify twenty years of Fascism in Italy!"[29]

Predictably, controversy ensued. On Saarinen's behalf, Hugh Ferriss—the legendary architectural delineator and a consultant to the Saarinens on the General Motors project—

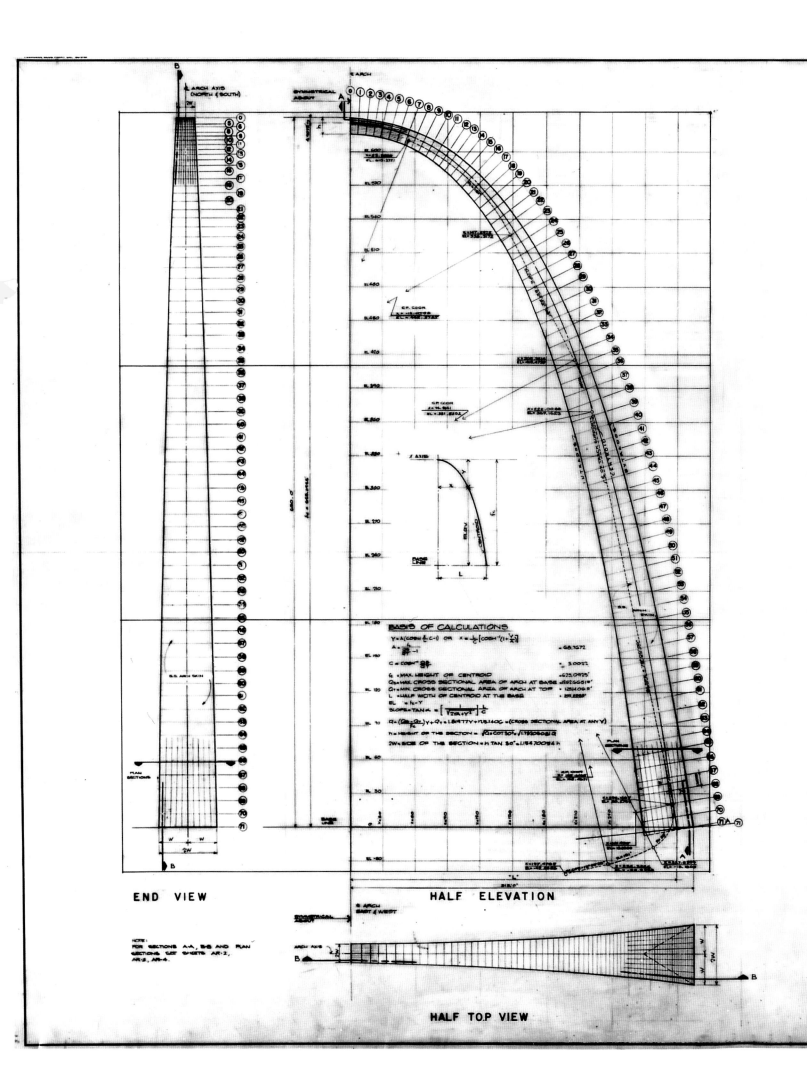

END VIEW

HALF ELEVATION

HALF TOP VIEW

BASIS OF CALCULATIONS

ARCH DATA

STATION	INTRADOS		CENTROID		EXTRADOS			CHORD	a	h	WALL THICKNESS
	X	EL	X	EL	X	EL	W				
0	0	642.7772	0	625.0972	0	630.00	8.5000	—	90°00'00"	14.7224	(.6354)

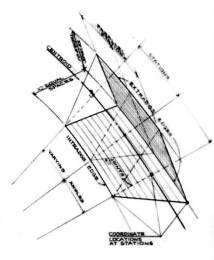

COORDINATE
LOCATIONS
AT STATIONS

INTENT OF GEOMETRY:

1. CENTROID IS DETERMINED BY FORMULA.

2. ALL SECTIONS PERPENDICULAR TO THE CENTROID ARE EQUILATERAL TRIANGLES.

3. THESE SECTIONS VARY IN AREA IN INVERSE PROPORTION TO THE ELEVATION OF THEIR CENTROIDS.

4. ALL EDGES FROM STATION 0 TO STATION 41 ARE SMOOTH CURVED LINES SUCH THAT ANY POINT ON THEM WILL SATISFY THE ABOVE GEOMETRY.

5. ALL EDGES FROM STATION 41 TO STATION 71 ARE CHORDS BETWEEN ADJACENT STATIONS SUCH THAT ANY POINT ON THE STATION WILL SATISFY THE ABOVE GEOMETRY.

(1) 71A IS THE THEORETICAL SECTION THRU X 315.0000 AND EL. 0.0000.
(2) 71 IS THE ACTUAL SECTION AT THE INTERSECTION OF THE ARCH AND THE RAMP.

ARCH GEOMETRY

JEFFERSON NATIONAL
EXPANSION MEMORIAL
ST. LOUIS   MISSOURI

UNITED STATES DEPARTMENT
OF THE INTERIOR
NATIONAL PARK SERVICE

EERO SAARINEN
AND ASSOCIATES
ARCHITECTS
BIRMINGHAM   MICHIGAN

RECOMMENDED

APPROVED

PRELIMINARY
CONSTRUCTION

DATE   ARCHITECT'S JOB NO.
10-16-61   5802

NNS-JNEM   SHEET NO.
3078   AR-1

ARCHITECT'S JOB NO. 5802
SHEET NO. AR-1

SCALE: 1" = 30'-0"
UNLESS OTHERWISE NOTED

DETAIL SYMBOL

wrote to Luther Ely Smith, chairman of the JNEM Association, arguing that, unlike Saarinen's design, Libera's arch was semicircular, and therefore it was ridiculous to describe Saarinen's arch as fascist. In spite of this and other similar testimonies in Saarinen's defense, Libera felt his rights had been infringed upon, and accused Saarinen of plagiarism. For his part, Saarinen denied any prior knowledge of Libera's design. "Nonsense" was the word he used to describe the controversy, according to a 1948 New York *Herald Tribune* article: "It's just preposterous to think that a basic form, formed completely on a natural figure, should have any ideological connection." Eventually the crisis was resolved when Wurster, after turning to the jury's comments, issued a statement declaring, "The form is in the public domain; it was not invented by the Fascists."[30]

The political atmosphere in 1948, just after World War II, was markedly different from today's. Now that more than five decades have passed, any fascist associations the arch may have had are gone. What remains reflects Saarinen's original vision: something "lofty, dynamic, of permanent significance," something that gives the park "a proper visual center," and as "the Gateway to the West," something that symbolizes "the spirit of the whole Memorial."[31]

ABOVE Esposizione Universale, Rome, 1942. Drawing by Giorgio Quaroni
RIGHT Gateway Arch, St. Louis, MO, 1948–64

SOCIALIZING

The total environment is the real problem and,
in a sense, the new frontier of architecture.

Architecture is inseparable from its social context. As Lewis Mumford has pointed out, works of architecture form a bridge between the private and the public, the individual and society: "Mind *takes form* in the city; and in turn, urban forms condition mind."[1] And so it is with certain characteristics of Saarinen's work.

Saarinen's concern for finding a balance between the private and the public in his architecture helps to explain his popularity as an architect and planner for educational institutions, which may be regarded as microcosms of urban life. In addition to his highly publicized commissions for Yale and MIT, Saarinen built dorms and other buildings at Drake University in Des Moines (1947–51), Stephens College in Columbia, Missouri (1953–57), Concordia Senior College in Fort Wayne, Indiana (1954–58), Vassar College in Poughkeepsie, New York (1954–58), the University of Chicago (1955–62), and the University of Pennsylvania (1957–60), and developed the North Campus Master Plan for the University of Michigan at Ann Arbor (1954), where he also built the School of Music (1962–64).

Similar concerns for the individual within a polity are evident in two corporate projects, both of which were designed in the postwar period when America was redefining its role domestically as well as internationally. The General Motors Technical Center in Warren, Michigan, represents an attempt to celebrate the image of a forward-looking manufacturing company within the context of a Detroit suburb at a time when that city was the epicenter of American ingenuity. The CBS Building exalts another private institution, integrating the broadcasting corporation into the urban fabric of Manhattan. Other Saarinen projects that manifest a similar approach to linking public and private include his American embassy buildings for London and Oslo, both of which balance their particular functions by thoroughly blending into the surrounding urban landscape.

Like so many modernists before him, Saarinen considered architecture an expression of the Zeitgeist. Giving form to "the awareness of the thinking and technology of our time" was an ever-present challenge for him, and he labored to use architecture as a vehicle for progress.[2] But he was also appreciative of the past. "Because we feel confident in our period, we can look at the past and derive inspiration instead of falling into imitation," he proclaimed in 1954.[3] This interest in belonging to the present while incorporating the heritage of the past—a foreshadowing of the postmodern condition—is radically different from the approach of the first-generation modernists, for whom the past was an oppressive construct to be overthrown.

By the mid-1950s in America, modernism, and especially the International Style, had become the normative idiom for corporate design. Saarinen expressed his own

view of the architecture of the day in an article titled "Six Broad Currents of Modern Architecture." Before breaking down the categories further, he described two groups of designers, the first comprising individualists, romanticists, and humanists (for instance, Frank Lloyd Wright, Alvar Aalto, and William Wurster), and the second, the classicists or functionalists, who followed in the line of Walter Gropius and Mies van der Rohe.

Of course, the architect who had the most direct bearing on Saarinen's work was his father. Echoing Wright's philosophy behind Broadacre City, the elder Saarinen regarded decentralization as the key to his urban philosophy. In his 1943 book *The City: Its Growth, Its Decay, Its Future*, he proposed a biological analogy, "organic decentralization," to describe urban transformation resulting in "grouping of new and reformed communities of adequate functional order according to the best principles of forward town-building."[4] Saarinen had several opportunities to collaborate with his father in urban projects, especially in the development of the university and college campuses at Drake and Stephens as well as at Antioch College in Yellow Springs, Ohio (1946–47) and Brandeis University in Waltham, Massachusetts (1948–50). The younger Saarinen devoted particular attention to campus organization and stressed the importance of master planning for future expansion. His North Campus Plan for Michigan examplifies an organizational scheme based on his father's concept of organic decentralization.

All of these influences—pragmatism, the International Style, the American tradition of innovation, and his father's organic urbanism—shaped the distinctively American environment in which Eero Saarinen practiced. The GM Technical Center and the CBS Building, two seminal projects in his body of work, illustrate his attempt to respond architecturally to the two most characteristic—and contrasting—sites in this American social context: the city and the suburb.

TOP Ingham Hall of Science, Drake University, Des Moines, IA, 1947–50
MIDDLE Law School, University of Chicago, Chicago, IL, 1955–58
BOTTOM Women's Dormitory, University of Chicago, Chicago, IL, 1955–58
RIGHT University of Michigan, Ann Arbor, MI, 1954. Master plan

DORMITORIES

NAT RESOURCES

DORMITORIES

FOOD
UNION

ENGINEERING

LIBRARY

FINE ARTS

RESEARCH

SERVICE

NORTH CAMPUS, UNIVERSITY OF MICHIGAN
ANN ARBOR, MICHIGAN
SITE PLAN F   SCALE 1"=200'
EERO SAARINEN & ASSOCIATES, ARCHITECTS

ABOVE Eero Saarinen with Aline Saarinen (right) at the dedication of the Emma Hartman Noyes House,
Vassar College, Poughkeepsie, NY, 1954–58
RIGHT Ingham Hall of Science, Drake University, Des Moines, IA, 1947–50
FOLLOWING SPREAD Saarinen Saarinen. Brandeis University, Waltham, MA, 1949–50

PREVIOUS SPREAD AND ABOVE Wyneken Hall, Concordia Senior College, Fort Wayne, IN, 1954–58
RIGHT Emma Hartman Noyes House, Vassar College, Poughkeepsie, NY, 1954–58

GENERAL MOTORS TECHNICAL CENTER
WARREN, MICHIGAN
1947–56

With a $100 million budget, the General Motors Technical Center, just outside of Detroit, was one of the largest architectural projects in postwar America. First proposed in 1944—by which point the burgeoning thirty-six-year-old company had already produced twenty-five million cars—the complex represented GM's desire to be at the forefront of technological research. It was an unprecedented investment in progress by private enterprise at a time when America, as writer Walter Lippmann stated, "had all the dynamism, all the innovation, all the crusading that human nature can take."[5]

The impetus for the project came from the corporation's vice president and director of research, Charles F. Kettering, and was backed by chairman Alfred P. Sloan. Envisioning a secluded campus environment where "tomorrow's challenge," as Kettering put it, could be taken up without distraction, they awarded the commission to Eliel Saarinen and his then partner, Robert Swanson. For the Saarinens, the commission represented "another Cranbrook," Eero Saarinen would later recount.[6] But the Saarinen and Swanson team made a case for a different kind of environment, one that would express the industrial character of the company's precision manufacturing mission. Rather than the homey, villagelike ensemble of buildings at Cranbrook, they proposed a series of low-lying, streamlined structures that would evoke the production-line efficiency of automotive assembly plants. Their first schemes for the site, which date from 1945, laid out the general guidelines for what would ultimately be built there. Instead of the romantic shapes that Eliel Saarinen usually employed, his early sketches for the GM project display a futuristic aesthetic.

It took three years from the time the first schemes were submitted—a period in which WWII would end, America would find itself in the midst of a vibrant economic expansion, and the notion that "what's good for GM is good for America" would be firmly instilled in the public imagination—before GM would fully commit itself, and the considerable resources required, to the proposed plan. Visionary Hugh Ferriss made the presentation drawings for the project. An illustrator and consulting architect, Ferriss had presented dramatic aerial and night views of the 350-acre plot and streamlined buildings. But finally, in 1948, after studying GM's long-range problems and reexamining its facilities, the project was resumed on a full-time basis. In the interim, Swanson had left the partnership with the Saarinens and Eero had replaced an ailing Eliel as lead architect on the project, and a new, expanded scheme had been developed under Eero's direction. Kettering and Sloan wholeheartedly embraced the new design and put the full range of the company's resources, technological and financial, at the Saarinens' disposal. As Kettering wrote, "Out of this appraisal has come a new conception—a Technical Center—a place where research, styling, advanced product study and process development can be brought together in one location, a place where each period of a long-time development can be considered separately—from the long-range developments of pure science to simple elements that would have their application tomorrow."[7]

Located 12 miles from Detroit on Mound Road, the Technical Center's half-square-mile site occupied one of the largest superblocks within the city's industrial belt. Yet despite its vast size and pristine condition at the time planning began, Saarinen worried that the tract could be jeopardized by its position inside the manufacturing zone if new plants were allowed to encroach.[8] A sprawling space unfettered by outside elements was essential to his vision of what the complex should be—an expansive yet self-contained arrangement of unified buildings within the landscape. From the outset, GM had stipulated that the center's five different functions (research, process development, engineering, styling, and service) be separated from one another in different buildings. This requirement, in addition to the need, given their proposed function, that the buildings be low rise, called for a horizontal program, which, in turn, made the site's apparently ample space suddenly seem limited.

Responding to these conditions, Saarinen laid out twenty-five buildings, none of which was more than three stories high, in five distinct groups. He situated them around three sides of a 22-acre lake and used a uniform vocabulary to "unite [them] visually as much as possible," he said in a project statement.[9] Along the perimeter he planted a forest of 13,000 trees to delimit and soften the seemingly endless array of angular glass and steel. This time it was Saarinen's associate J. Henderson Barr who made many of the presentation drawings for the finally 320 acres of the ensemble, showing overall views and details of the different sections.[10]

With the central "water wall" fountain and rhythmic sequence of the curtain glass facade broken only by the irregular form of a stainless steel water tower and the gleaming metal dome of the styling complex's auditorium, the Technical Center evinced a certain magisterial quality. Its imperial scale, repetition of motifs, and emphasis on perspectival axes, which led to comparisons with the baroque urbanism of Louis Le Vau and the landscaping of André Lenôtre, inspired a 1956 *Architectural Forum* article in which the complex was dubbed an "industrial Versailles."[11] The center's setting, dominated by an immense reflecting pool, suggests analogies to another kind of stately space: the public plaza. Like Washington's National Mall, designed in 1901 after Charles L'Enfant's eighteenth-century plan, the Technical Center's expansive and lushly planted terrain, punctuated with incidental and monumental structures, creates a sublime environment in the midst of a large city.

ABOVE Eliel Saarinen and Robert Swanson. GMTC, Warren, MI, 1945
Saarinen and Swanson's project presentation
RIGHT GMTC, Warren, MI, 1947–56. Master plan, drawn by J. Henderson Barr

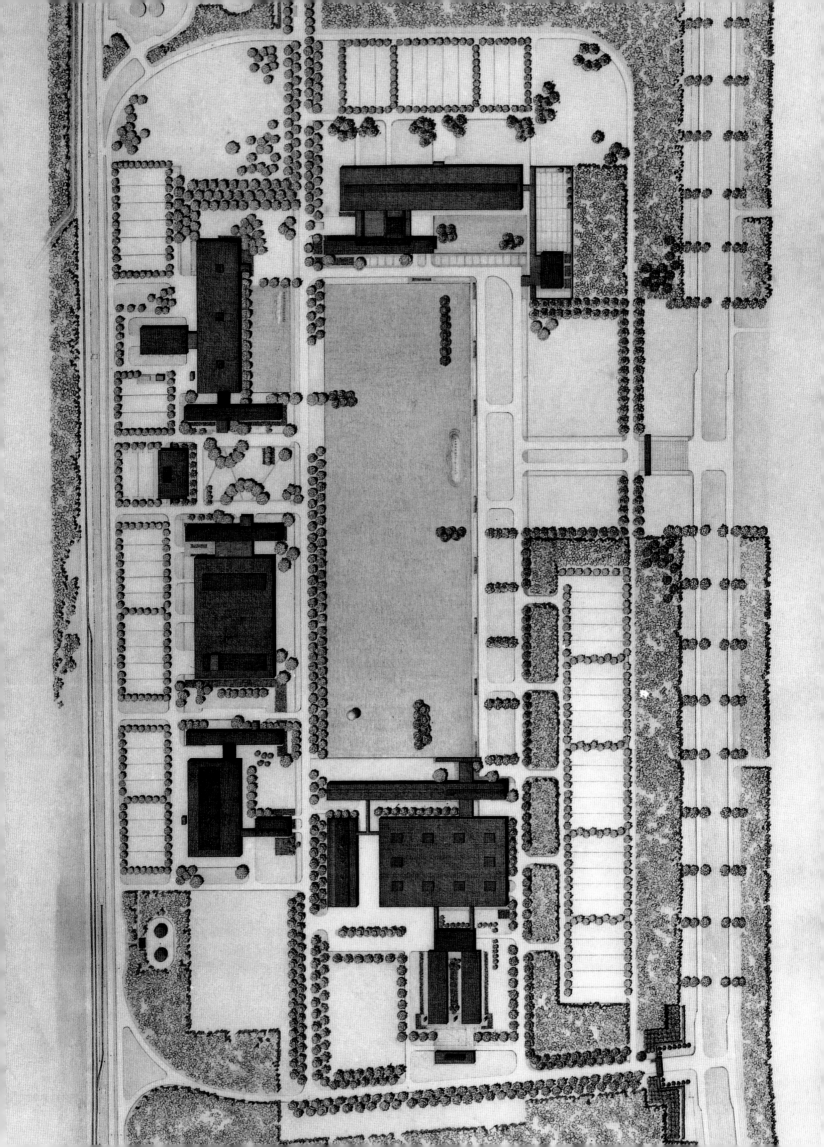

ABOVE GMTC, Warren, MI, 1947–56. Renderings by J. Henderson Barr

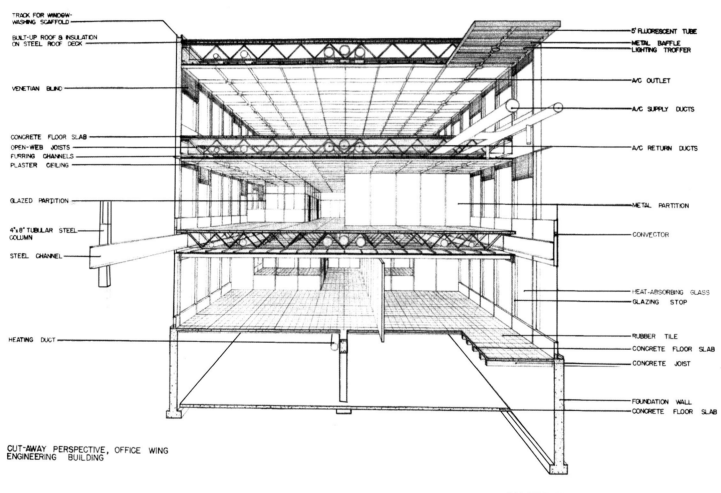

TRACK FOR WINDOW-
WASHING SCAFFOLD

BUILT-UP ROOF & INSULATION
ON STEEL ROOF DECK

VENETIAN BLIND

CONCRETE FLOOR SLAB
OPEN-WEB JOISTS
FURRING CHANNELS
PLASTER CEILING

GLAZED PARTITION

4"x8" TUBULAR STEEL
COLUMN

STEEL CHANNEL

HEATING DUCT

5' FLUORESCENT TUBE
METAL BAFFLE
LIGHTING TROFFER

A/C OUTLET

A/C SUPPLY DUCTS

A/C RETURN DUCTS

METAL PARTITION

CONVECTOR

HEAT-ABSORBING GLASS
GLAZING STOP

RUBBER TILE
CONCRETE FLOOR SLAB
CONCRETE JOIST

FOUNDATION WALL
CONCRETE FLOOR SLAB

CUT-AWAY PERSPECTIVE, OFFICE WING
ENGINEERING BUILDING

G.M. TECHNICAL CENTER
SAARINEN, SAARINEN AND ASSOCIATES · 4807
SMITH, HINCHMAN AND GRYLLS

ABOVE GMTC, Warren, MI, 1947–56. Engineering section

If the baroque palace served as one source of inspiration and the eighteenth-century plaza another, Saarinen's main referent for the Technical Center was certainly the modern industrial complex. The strict functionalist vocabulary, the deliberate inclusion of mechanisms that subtly interrupt the seemingly rigid symmetry, and the overlapping arrangement of elements all suggest that the real roots of his design are to be found in modernism, specifically in the work of Albert Kahn and Mies van der Rohe. Indeed, Saarinen made no secret of his debt to Kahn's industrial aesthetic or Mies's pared-down formalism.

Having introduced Eliel Saarinen to the Michigan academic community, Kahn had become a close friend of the family when they settled at Cranbrook. During his most formative years, the younger Saarinen took great interest in Kahn's industrial-belt buildings for companies such as Ford, Chrysler, and General Motors. Saarinen admired the *Sachlichkeit* Kahn brought to the city and his inventive facility with steel, but found fault with Kahn's treatment of the administration buildings in these industrial complexes: "He never saw the administration building as a part of the total group, for instance. But he did use steel well," Saarinen commented. At GM, as if in response, Saarinen seamlessly integrated administration areas with other offices, research facilities, and factory shops.

Mies was never an intimate friend of Eero Saarinen's, but his work had an even more pronounced influence on the Technical Center than Kahn's. "I was personally at the time very influenced by Mies van der Rohe's Illinois Tech Buildings—the purity of the shape and the clear expression of the structure," Saarinen said.[12] The simplicity of organization and masses, the application of the orthogonal axis, and the exclusivity of industrialized materials are just a few of the Miesian elements Saarinen included in his proposal for GM. Saarinen's decision to reduce his own formal invention to a minimum and emulate Mies's well-established canonic vocabulary was a deliberate way of conferring status or elevating the proposal from industrial park to stately campus.

It was also a way of coping with the titanic scale of the superblock. As theorist Alan Colquhoun remarked in his 1981 text *The Superblock*, buildings of such gargantuan proportions defy metaphor. "The architect has either to rely on a cybernetic model of randomness or to invent a vocabulary which in some degree refers to the traditional language of architecture."[13] Clearly Saarinen chose the latter path with his adaptation of Miesian uniformity. But at 320 acres the Technical Center was nearly three times the size of the 120-acre IIT campus, and Saarinen understood that size made all the difference; he knew that without some internal variation, the massive complex would come across as a lifeless monolith, unbearably dull to look at and terribly confusing to navigate.

ABOVE GMTC, Warren, MI 1947–56. Ezra Stoller © Esto

Saarinen devised various strategies for introducing differentiation among the five building zones and within the buildings themselves. One involved tiling the end wall of every building in a different color. With vivid hues such as deep crimson, bright scarlet, sky blue, tangerine orange, lemon yellow, acidic chartreuse, royal blue, tobacco gray, and chocolate brown, the glazed bricks, which were developed specially for the Technical Center project, added personality to the drafting, administration, and laboratory buildings, and the shops and special-use spaces.[14] In contrast to the buildings' blue-gray glass facades, the bold wall treatments endowed each structure with a distinct identity.

The streamlined water tower also helped break up the monotony of the repetitive and boxy forms. "Against the desperately long horizontal lines was needed a vertical," Saarinen admitted. "The water tower gave us this."[15] Because of its three-stem support, elongated shape, and strategic position in the lake, this tower served as a kind of general counterpoint to the low-slung architecture throughout the complex. Evidence of a tower was already apparent in Eliel Saarinen's first proposal, but nearly twenty models were made before the team arrived at a final design.

With two fanciful fountains and four small islands adorned by willow trees, the central lake provided another kind of visual counterpoint. The first fountain, a 50-foot-high, 115-foot-wide wall of water, was designed to face the Mound Road gate. The second, by Alexander Calder, was designed with variable speed and sound as a "mobile fountain sculpture." With changing spray patterns creating different motifs (which Calder named "Fantails," "Seven Sisters," "Plops," and "Scissors"), the fountain's water play offered a means of constant visual diversity. A third fountain, in the pool by the styling section's administration building, and a nearby bronze sculpture, *Flight of the Bird*, by Antoine Pevsner, are additional features that subtly offset the symmetry and repetition of the complex.[16]

The buildings were also differentiated internally. In the research section's administration building, for example, Saarinen designed a particularly elaborate interior scheme. His plans for the lobby, which he conceived as an exhibition area, specify a different furniture arrangement and color scheme than used elsewhere in the complex. Unique features, such as a curved reception desk, a double-height entry, and a spiral staircase suspended on stainless steel rods, gave the whole room a distinctive sculptural quality.[17] Another extraordinary interior was created in the central restaurant building, which featured a spectacular 36-by-10-foot gold-colored metal screen by frequent Saarinen collaborator Harry Bertoia.

The one building on the GM campus Saarinen designed as a unique form, both internally and externally, was the domed auditorium in the styling section. Conceived as a multipurpose room, 65 feet high at its apex and 188 feet wide, it served as a projection space, a reception hall for banquets, and a space for automobile display and study. Saarinen's idea that an automobile should be observed in natural light led him to propose the domed shape, which could be indirectly lit. Built with the same two-ply stressed-skin construction technique he used for the Jefferson National Expansion Memorial, the dome's inner layer was assembled with perforated 1/8-inch-thick steel plates. For the outer shell, Saarinen covered the welded 3/8-inch-thick steel plates with insulating material and then sheathed the whole body with aluminum.[18]

Of the Technical Center's twenty-five different structures, the office building in the engineering section was the first to be built. As such, it was the site of the first trials for many of Saarinen's innovative internal designs, including a revolutionary air-conditioning system that was integrated into the ceiling and a newly scaled module that would become standard for offices around the world. Comprised of 4-by-8-inch perimeter steel columns and 50-by-2.5-foot trusses, the building's three-level structure was specially designed with open interior passages to accommodate high-velocity air-conditioning ducts and lighting fixtures. Though standard practice today, the structural integration of climate control systems was completely novel at the time, as was the 5-foot-2-inch module, now widely used, that Saarinen developed in response to GM's request for larger-than-standard offices. Because the company stipulated that no office should be smaller than 10-by-15 feet, Saarinen found himself unable to use the typical 4-by-3-foot module: two modules were too small for the smallest office, but three made the space too large. Standard issue, 5-foot-long fluorescent lighting tubes were another constraint. In order to accommodate the integrated ceiling system, which had to take into account not only the structure and mechanical installations, but also the tubular lights, the module needed to be bigger than normal. As Kevin Roche explained, it was the first time that anyone had combined the structural, mechanical, lighting, and layout modules in a modern structure.[19]

The building's facade was conceived as a curtain wall and clearly follows the guidelines Mies van der Rohe introduced in IIT's Alumni Memorial Hall (1945). Its hollow steel columns, disposed according to the 5-foot-2-inch module, act as mullions supporting the glass-and-metal panels arranged between them. Insulation was the principle concern in the glass design. Saarinen's solution involved attaching a heat-absorbing, 1/4-inch-thick plate to the exterior and a similarly thick clear plate to the interior, leaving a shallow air space in between. For the opaque panels, he turned to a new product: the prefabricated metal sandwich panel.[20] Made of porcelain enamel steel skin bonded to a heavy Kraft paper honeycomb core and filled with granular insulation, this panel easily met the insulation requirements of the wall.

While the fundamental elements—module size, ceiling and climate control integration, and curtain wall insulation—were established in the complex's initial building, Saarinen continued to modify certain features as construction proceeded. For example, in the research center's administration building, he made a major improvement in the curtain wall with a neoprene gasket weather seal for glass and sandwich panels. Commonly used in bus and car windshields, this type of seal had never been used in a building. Frank Lloyd Wright had employed a gasket system in the glass tubing wall of his Johnson Wax Company in Racine, Wisconsin (1936–50), but here the joints were "zipped" by a neoprene filler strip that compressed the seal, enabling the assembly to withstand winds of up to 120 miles per hour. Meanwhile, the first sandwich panels were also improved. Bonding the honeycomb paper core to the steel skin had become a problem. The glue was not strong enough to keep the porcelain and steel from separating. In response, Saarinen proposed a new adhesive and aluminum panels.[21]

Each of Saarinen's innovations, from macro to micro, was part of a larger effort on his part to give the complex a civic character. More than just a graceful version of the standard industrial complex, he saw the GM project as a chance to design a productive and enriching community for the four thousand workers who would spend their days there. According to his model, it would be a place where people could come together to work out not just what the next sedan might look like, but what the very idea of future productivity might entail. Thus he configured the state-of-the-art facilities to promote exchange and added authentic artistic creations and beautifully landscaped grounds for inspiration. As such, the complex became—much more than a mere reflection of industrial enterprise—an expression of postindustrial society, which, as sociologist Daniel Bell wrote, "is organized around knowledge, for the purpose of social control and the directing of innovation and change."[22]

COLUMBIA BROADCASTING SYSTEM (CBS) BUILDING
NEW YORK, NEW YORK
1960–65

In striking contrast to the suburban horizontality of his General Motors Technical Center, Saarinen's CBS Building took form as a towering vertical in the dense urbanity of midtown Manhattan. It was his first, and only, skyscraper.

In July of 1960, CBS—then under the stewardship of chairman William S. Paley and president Frank Stanton—announced plans to build a new headquarters in New York City. The company wanted a modern building, but one that would stand out from the prosaic skyscrapers that had become ubiquitous in the 1950s. Saarinen was the obvious choice, given his unconventional trajectory, and he eagerly accepted the commission. "I am excited," he announced upon formally taking on the project. "The challenge here is a form that expresses the creative, dynamic spirit of electronic communications. The subject is not tame." Nor were his ambitions. Sadly, he only had time to outline the design before his death in September of 1961. The elaboration and completion of the plans was left to his collaborators.[23]

The site, fronting Sixth Avenue between Fifty-second and Fifty-third Streets, was within blocks of the RCA Building (home of rival NBC) and the new headquarters of Time Inc., among other towers. Given the bustling locale, Saarinen envisioned a simple tower—"a soaring thing"—that would be set back from the avenue and accompanied by a sunken, tree-lined plaza where people would find a calm respite amidst the city's frenzied streets.[24]

The role played by architecture as a mediator between the social and economic activities of a city is reflected in its building codes. When Saarinen began work on his proposal, New York City was in the process of reformulating its zoning regulations, which, having been established in 1916, were egregiously outdated. Unprecedented at the time they were introduced and subsequently adopted by numerous American cities, the pioneering legislation led to the stepped setback or "wedding-cake" form that defined some of the city's—and indeed the world's—most iconic skyscrapers, such as the Empire State and Chrysler buildings. Yet, by the late 1940s, the city's postwar affluence had ignited a massive building boom, and the need to overhaul the outdated regulations had become obvious. As a 1950 *Architectural Forum* article reported: "Its bulk restrictions have proven tight as an iron cakemold, but its land use and density restrictions have proven loose as a billowing circus tent." Thus, a special rezoning study was begun, and in 1961 a new resolution was passed. The new rules no longer rewarded step-back construction, instead favoring tower-in-the-plaza schemes. In order to gain the support of the real-estate industry, a measure stipulating that a building floor area could be as large as the site area multiplied by fifteen (FAR 15) was allowed in commercial districts.[25]

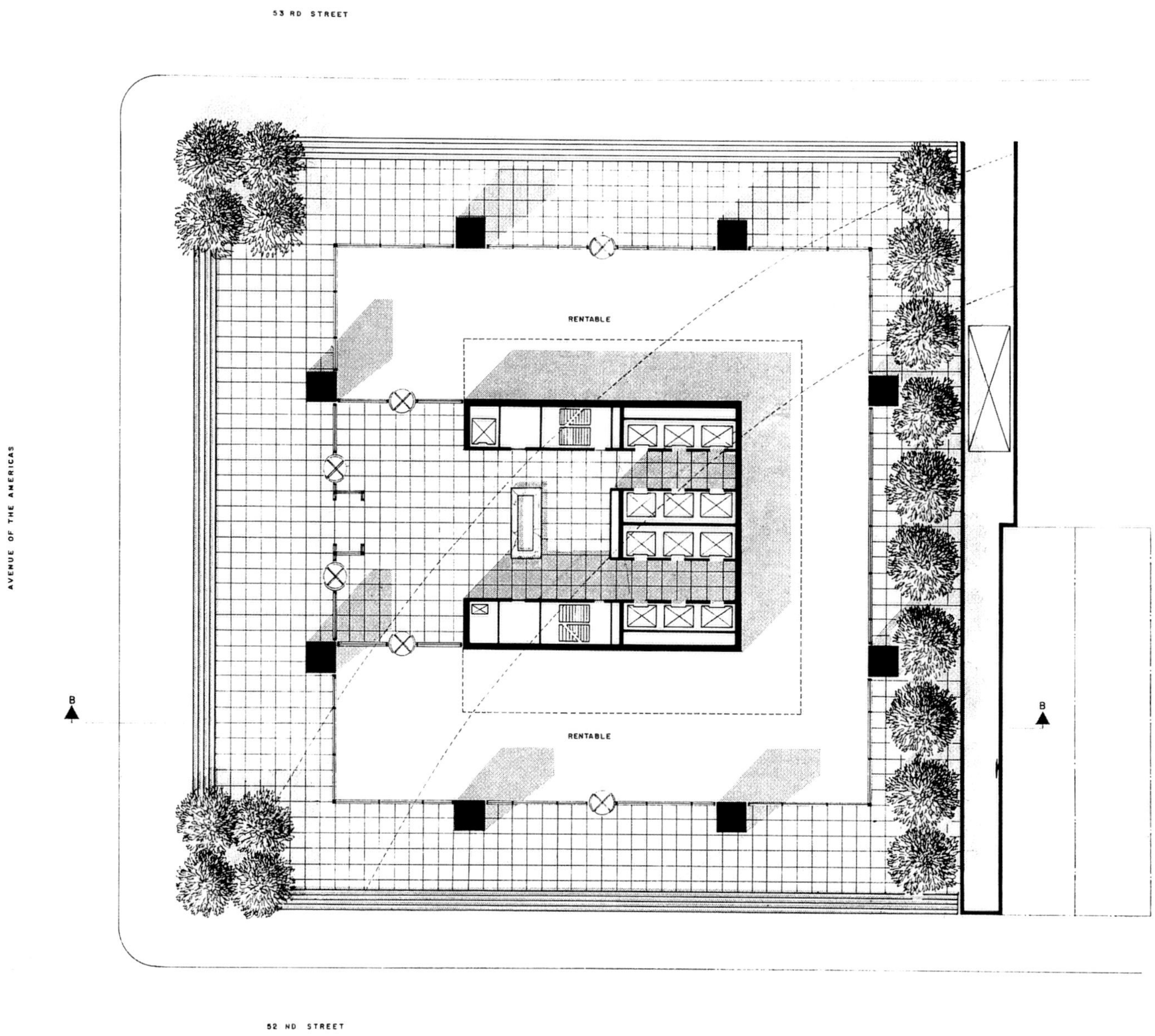

53 RD STREET

AVENUE OF THE AMERICAS

RENTABLE

RENTABLE

B

B

52 ND STREET

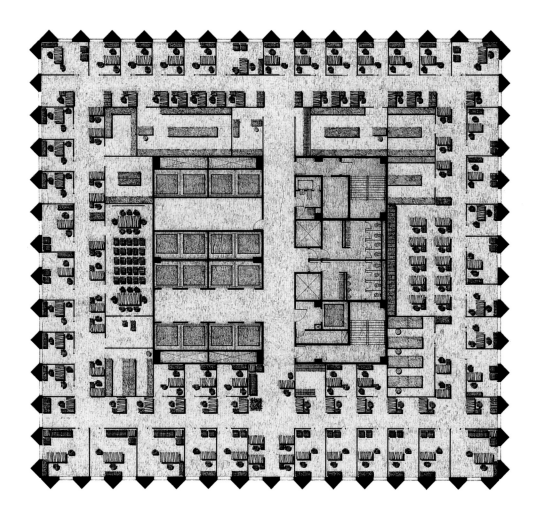

Saarinen's plan for the CBS Building, which was situated in the middle of the restricted central commercial district, was directly influenced by these new zoning laws. Having worked closely with City Planning Commissioner James Felt from the outset of the project in 1960, Saarinen knew that his proposal would have to conform to the impending ordinance.[26] Axonometric diagrams, drawn by Saarinen's office in August 1961 show five possible alternatives for the CBS Building that, with a site area of 47,696 square feet, would allow for a maximum floor area of 715,440 square feet according to the FAR 15 formula. To check the bulk effect on adjacent buildings, these concepts were converted into models. One had the building fully covering the site, which limited it to fifteen floors. Another showed a partially occupied site in which a single tower rose thirty-eight floors. A version of this scheme was ultimately adopted for the building.

In the final design, the building was set back 28 feet from Sixth Avenue, leaving room for a subgrade public space. Such open areas, or "urban plazas," were strongly encouraged by the new resolution's "incentive zoning" program, in which developers were offered bonus floor space if plazas were included in their proposals. The public character of the CBS Building's plaza was limited by being five steps below the sidewalk. Yet like similar spaces in midtown, the granite-clad pit did constitute a calm, if somewhat forbidding, place to rest in the midst of New York's frenzy.

For Saarinen, the plaza also functioned as a kind of inverted pedestal upon which his building could be properly viewed. It created breathing room and a sense of perspective between the streetscape and the structure that was critical, in Saarinen's opinion, for human-scale urban development. "We tried to place the building on the site so that we could have a plaza and still not destroy the street line....A plaza is a very necessary thing in a city. It lets people sit in the sun and look at the sky. A plaza allows a building to be seen."[27]

With a 125-by-155-foot floor plan, the CBS tower is rectangular in form. Of the five models Saarinen's office built, all but one showed square-shaped structures, which suggests that the rectangle was not Saarinen's ideal solution. According to Kevin Roche, who led the design team after Saarinen's death, the search for efficiency in the layout freed the plan from the need for traditional service corridors around the central elevator core. "What Eero wanted to do," Roche said, "was to make a core where everything was entered from the elevator portion, so the perimeter around it didn't need to be penetrated, which meant that then you could increase the amount of usable space ... and make a more efficient plan."[28] The resulting layout provided for a 55-by-85-

foot core with sixteen elevators in four banks. Throughout the structure, Saarinen employed a 5-square-foot module similar to the one he devised for the General Motors Technical Center, which permitted 10-square-foot divisions.

As a single, soaring tower, Saarinen's design related formally to skyscrapers built prior to the 1961 ordinance, such as Eliel Saarinen's proposal for the Chicago Tribune competition (1922), or Louis Sullivan's Guaranty Building in Buffalo, New York (1896). Admittedly, Saarinen was mindful of Sullivan's conception when he undertook the project: "I wanted a building that would be a soaring thing. I think Louis Sullivan was right to want the skyscraper to be a soaring thing," he said in 1961.[29] Saarinen dispensed with the tripartite, base-shaft-cap division that Sullivan had used in his skyscrapers, however, making the CBS Building a more contemporary expression of modern design. Even the entry was understated to the point of near invisibility.

Typological considerations in Saarinen's design reflected formal and functional concerns as well as structural ones. In the 1950s, skyscrapers were generally built with steel structures, but as Kevin Roche has pointed out, by the beginning of the 1960s, it had begun to be viable to build them in concrete.[30] Accordingly, engineer Paul Weidlinger, who was responsible for the structure, proposed a reinforced concrete system based on a perimeter bearing wall for the tower's massive frame. With 5-foot-wide, V-shaped columns arranged according to a 10-foot module, and a 55-by-85-foot core bearing wall, the structure could accommodate slab floors and an open plan. Engineer William LeMessurier has noted the peculiarity of this structural arrangement. Whereas the perimeter structure usually acts as a frame with internal columns taking care of the structural requirements, in the CBS Building the perimeter structure was used as a bearing wall with the structural requirements—including bracing capacity for wind and earthquake—being met by the spatial arrangement of the elements. (A similar system, using steel, was employed in the World Trade Center.[31])

The columns also provided a safe way of integrating the internal systems. While the air-conditioning, water, and heating were centralized on the second and twenty-eighth floors, their ducts and pipes ran through the interior of the columns throughout the building. Further, the shape of the column, a sort of wedge, allowed for more light from different angles than conventionally shaped columns, making a brighter workspace with better sight lines from the building. Saarinen knew that the angled columns, clad in Canadian black granite, would be the building's distinguishing feature, giving the tower a unique appearance as well as a fortified structure.[32] Special attention was given to the stone's rough texture, which was treated first with a burning technique

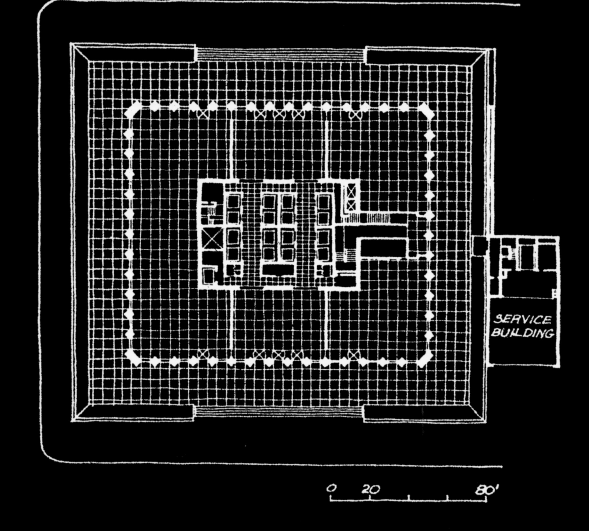

SERVICE
BUILDING

0   20   80'

ABOVE AND RIGHT CBS Building, New York, NY, 1960–64. Plan and section

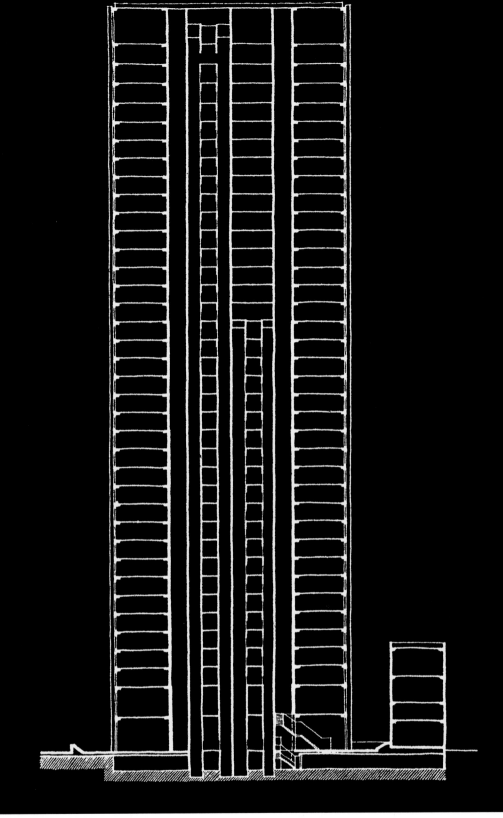

called "thermal stippling" and then with a blasting method called "liquid honing," in which the surface was sprayed with a slurry of water and abrasive. In fact, when seen at an angle, the V-shaped pillars tend to conceal the windows, making the whole building look like a solid block of black granite. It was just this effect that led to the building's nickname, "Black Rock."

The CBS Building represented a radical alternative to the glass-and-steel towers in the tradition established by Mies van der Rohe. For many critics, this departure was nothing less than shocking. The very concept of a thirty-eight-story concrete tower, especially one with no reduction of column mass in the upper floors, garnered heavy criticism. And then there was the fact that the corner columns were not strictly necessary. These extraneous features were unacceptable to dogmatic modernists who demanded strict structural honesty.[33]

But for Saarinen, who never fully subscribed to any one architectural ideology, expression was always part of the formula, whether he was designing a hockey rink, a college dorm, or a national monument. "I believe the spirit of a building should be expressed, not hidden behind a neutral curtain of glass. Buildings should have 'guts' and direction and make statements," he said. Exaggerating the CBS structure's solidity was just one way of expressing the tower's singular simplicity—something Saarinen aspired to above all: "Its beauty will be, I believe, that it will be the simplest skyscraper statement in New York," he predicted.[34]

The interior decor, which was assigned to the firm of Carson, Lundin and Shaw, translated the purist lines Saarinen envisioned for the building's exterior into colors and shapes that animated its interior. The furniture commission went to the Knoll Planning Unit, then under the direction of Florence Knoll, who had been a contemporary of Saarinen's at Cranbrook. In collaboration with Carson, Lundin and Shaw, Knoll selected furniture, fabrics, colors, paintings, and sculptures: "My real job was the proper assembly of everything," she said. That the resulting scheme echoed the building's minimalist character was considered contrived by certain critics.[35]

Though he didn't live to see it, such internal and external consistency perfectly conveyed Saarinen's vision for the tower. His main concern was to create a corporate image that would distinguish CBS in the media and physical landscapes. Thus he balanced the company's desire for "permanence, dignity, and strength," with expressive, untraditional elements designed to both reveal and conceal the corporation's strategy for thriving in the knowledge-based, postindustrial context of early 1960s urban New York.

RIGHT CBS Building, New York, NY, 1960–65

JUDGING

Continual reevaluation is necessary. We must constantly question the validity of many of our practices.

An architect is the judge of his own works as well as those of others. But judgment does not come without cost. In discussing the link between contemporary architectural practice and criticism, Robert Venturi pinpointed a certain loss of innocence: "Architects today are too educated to be either primitive or totally spontaneous, and architecture is too complex to be approached with carefully maintained ignorance."[1] In critiquing his own projects and those of his peers, Saarinen contributed to the creation of a culture of intense self-scrutiny and competitiveness that has radically transformed the profession of architecture over the last half century.

Saarinen was a born competitor. As a student at Yale University he won numerous prizes in the so-called Beaux Arts competitions among the various architectural schools. Throughout his career he tried to win not only commissions and awards, but also seats on juries and prize committees. His colleagues often testified to Saarinen's competitive side, as did the architectural press. A 1962 *Architectural Forum* profile titled "Eero Saarinen: A Complete Architect" made a point of remarking on his ambition. Saarinen's particular combination of competitive and collaborative proclivities ranks him alongside other successful designers of his generation, most notably Gordon Bunshaft of Skidmore, Owings & Merrill. [2]

In 1939 Saarinen and his father jointly won the competition for the Smithsonian Gallery of Art in Washington, DC. Two years later Saarinen collaborated with Charles Eames to win the "Organic Design in Home Furnishings" competition organized by the Museum of Modern Art, establishing his reputation as a furniture designer. In 1944 he teamed with Oliver L. Lundquist to win first prize in a competition organized by *Arts & Architecture* to develop houses of limited size that would be suitable for postwar mass construction. But the signal competition of Saarinen's career was the 1947 contest for the Jefferson National Expansion Memorial in Saint Louis. Also noteworthy are Saarinen's winning entry in the 1956 competition for the United States Embassy in London and his second prize in the 1960 competition for the World Health Organization headquarters in Geneva.

Saarinen's approach to competitions, both as a judge and as a participant, is relevant to a consideration of his activity as a critic. He was a relentless advocate of "chasing the problems," believing that "once you have caught them, you can always solve them." His competitiveness was a sign of his ongoing effort to get to the bottom of problems in his own work. As evidenced in the case of his United States embassy building in London, no amount of self-scrutiny and revision thwarted his critical drive. Likewise, discerning the essence of a problem was for him the main task of any competition judgment. He always attached particular importance to the composition of the jury: "Who is the strong man?" he would ask, and, "What will stimulate him?" He was convinced that one judge on any given jury would usually prevail, and he liked to be that dominant figure. The Sydney Opera House competition provides an interesting example and may be an exception to that rule. But as a critic of his contemporaries, Saarinen did not demonstrate his positions though a strict critical analysis. He reacted to the work of his contemporaries, to use Robert Venturi's words, "as an architect who employs criticism rather than as a critic who chooses architecture."[3]

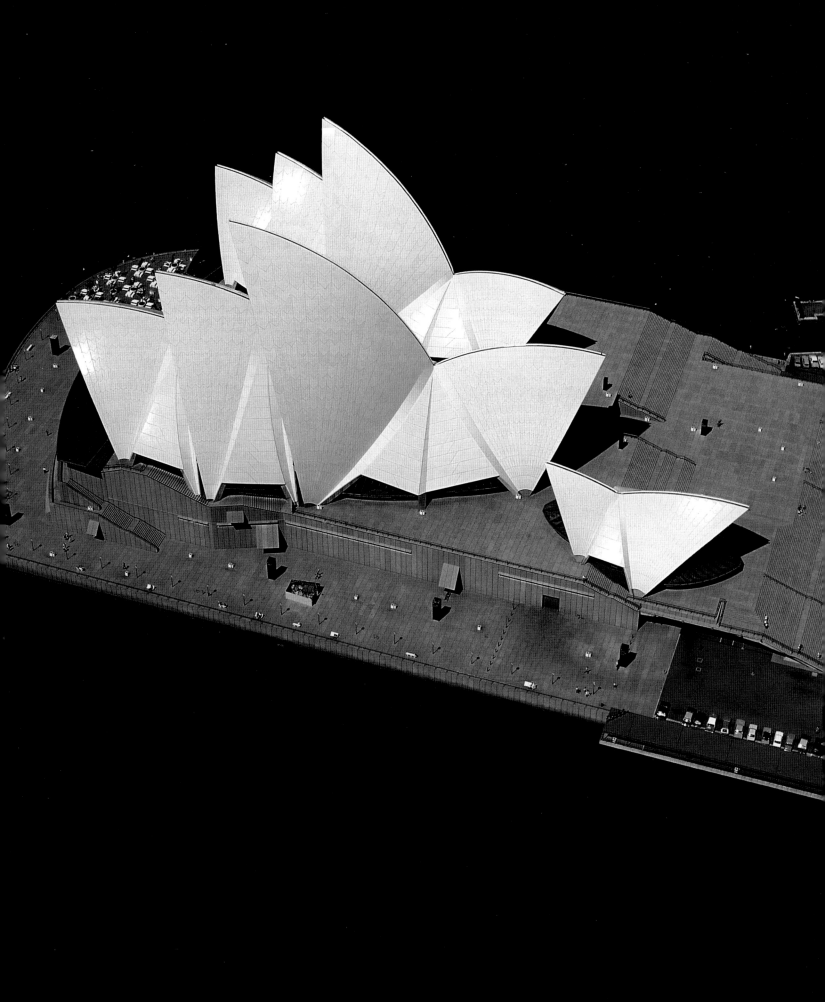

THE SYDNEY OPERA HOUSE COMPETITION
1957

As the architectural historian Philip Drew has described in great detail, the driving force behind the Sydney Opera House construction project was conductor Eugene Goosens, who was backed by John Joseph Cahill, the Labor politician and New South Wales premier. Bennelong Point in Sydney Harbor was selected as the site of the new structure that would incorporate two auditoriums seating 3,500 and 1,200 people. The terms of the international design competition were announced in January 1956. One year later, a jury was convened. It included four architects: professor H. Ingham Ashworth of the University of Sydney; Cobden Parkes, the New South Wales government architect; Dr. Leslie Martin, from the United Kingdom; and Eero Saarinen, from the United States. From 230 submitted designs and seventeen shortlisted projects, the proposal by Danish architect Jørn Utzon was declared the winner on 29 January 1957.[4]

The jury report laid out some preliminary considerations about the jurors' preferences: "The Assessors have proceeded by considering all the schemes submitted from the point of view of siting, the internal circulation and planning, and finally from the point of view of whether the resulting building will have an architectural significance.... We have been impressed by the beauty and the exceptional possibilities of the site in relation to the harbor and we are convinced that the silhouette of any proposed building is of the greatest importance."[5] With reference to Utzon's winning submission, the jury pointed out:

> The drawings submitted for this scheme are simple to the point of being diagrammatic. Nevertheless, as we have returned again and again to the study of these drawings, we are convinced that they present a concept of an Opera House which is capable of becoming one of the great buildings of the world. We consider this scheme to be the most original and creative submission. Because of its very originality, it is clearly a controversial design. We are, however, absolutely convinced about its merits.[6]

Although the report suggests that standard judging procedures were followed, some historians are convinced that Saarinen played a decisive role in the final decision. The critic Sigfried Giedion wrote in 1964 that Saarinen, having arrived several days late to the deliberations, picked up Utzon's drawings from the stack of rejected projects and declared: "Gentlemen, this is the first prize."[7] The anecdote has been repeated far and wide; its veracity, however, has been questioned by at least one of the jurors, H. I. Ashworth. As Drew suggests, one of the main reasons for this element of doubt must have been Professor Ashworth's sense of expediency when defending, as chairman of the jury, the collective nature of the decision.

LEFT AND FOLLOWING SPREAD Jørn Utzon. Sydney Opera House, Sydney, Australia, 1957–73

Saarinen's exact role will never be confirmed. But given his strong powers of persuasion, there is little doubt that he had a decisive influence. Certainly, it took a great leap of imagination to discern the genius of Utzon's proposal. The competition rules established that neither perspective color drawings nor models could be entered. Utzon's line drawings themselves were so basic that they gave rise to speculation as to whether they were even finished, or whether he had entered the competition with any hope of winning. Furthermore, they were up against far more elaborate proposals of rival teams. That it would have taken an architect with considerable design skills to envisage Utzon's schematic project in full lends credence to Drew's speculation that Saarinen and juror Leslie Martin held sway over the panel's decision.[8]

Additional evidence of Saarinen's primacy on the panel lies in a pair of drawings that he dedicated to Cahill.[9] These vivid sketches, rendered quickly with chalk and charcoal, describe how Utzon's proposal would look in Sydney Harbor—a perspective that was far from clear based on Utzon's submission. One drawing corresponds to the west elevation, showing the Opera House and its reflection in the water; the second highlights the location of the proposal at Bennelong Point. The drawings exhibit Saarinen's belief in the proposal, and while we don't know if they helped rescue Utzon's project from the reject pile, they leave little doubt as to the force of Saarinen's persuasion in the course of the deliberations.

Next to "the general breadth of the imaginative concept," the jury identified "unity of structural expression" as an essential criterion in making the selection, and this, too, may be seen as a reflection of Saarinen's concerns. In lauding Utzon's "great simplicity of arrangement," the jury report echoed a sentiment voiced by Saarinen in 1957, that the "challenge of making a building a total expression seems to me the highest and most difficult one."[10] And there were other clearly identifiable connections between the outlook of the two architects—most notably when it came to parallels between the Sydney Opera House and Saarinen's own TWA Terminal.

Saarinen and Roche's model for TWA predated the Sydney decision, and as such suggests that Saarinen's work on the terminal might have been influential in the choice of Utzon. There are also strong affinities between the Opera House and Saarinen's Kresge Auditorium at MIT, a building already finished in 1955. The April 1957 drawings on Saarinen's desk calendar suggest that the development of Saarinen's shells for the TWA Terminal might have been influenced by the Opera House. This is not to suggest that Saarinen was the only jury member who supported Utzon's design. The jury report clearly observed that "the technique of building shell vaults has now been developed in many countries of the world; in particular in the United States, Italy, England, Germany and Brazil. The use of this form of construction seems to us to be particularly appropriate." Nevertheless, the affinity between the work of the two architects further underscores the likelihood of Saarinen's pivotal role in Utzon's selection.[11]

The jury report anticipated that the design for the Opera House would be "open to many points of detailed criticism and a number of corrections would have to be made." Two opposing positions stand out from the many judgments delivered by critics. Among the project's supporters, Sigfried Giedion adhered to a cyclical vision of history and perceived Utzon as the most prominent member of a third generation of modern architects that included Moshe Safdie, Kisho Kurokawa, James Stirling, Venturi & Rauch, and Roche & Dinkeloo. In a 1964 article, Giedion listed several characteristics of the group, including an emphasis on the horizontal plane, a stronger relationship with the past, the strengthening of sculptural tendencies, and the supremacy of expression over pure function.[12]

The counterpoint to Giedion's enthusiastic support was provided by Félix Candela, an architect and builder who was particularly critical of Utzon's achievement. In a widely discussed 1967 article, Candela scrutinized the development of the project in great detail, focusing on the feasibility of its construction. Candela echoed the opinions of Pier Luigi Nervi and other critics of the plan who, from the outset, had questioned its practical viability. The crux of Candela's criticism was that the plan was conceived without much regard for how the opera house would actually be built. To be sure, there were valid concerns. Not long after the jury handed down its decision, circumstances conspired to throw the project in doubt: a loss of confidence in Utzon, owing to a change of government; difficulties encountered by engineer Ove Arup in executing the shell construction; and the balooning of the budget, from 7.5 to 60 million Australian dollars. "The obvious mistake was to underestimate the influence that scale or size has in every structural problem," Candela protested. Although his criticism has since been eclipsed by Sydney's tremendous success, Candela's contempt for the jury is worthy of note.[13]

Despite the threat of criticism, the jury could not hide its enthusiasm: "It is difficult to think of a better silhouette for this peninsula," the panel gushed; concerns about the feasibility of the shell construction were not addressed.[14] What might now be seen as excessive confidence in shell technique led the jury to base its decision solely on the formal expression and creativity of Utzon's proposal. This choice certainly reveals the hand of Saarinen, a staunch advocate of structural experimentation. Indeed, Saarinen's influence in Sydney should be regarded as one of the decisive interventions in the architecture of the second half of the twentieth century.

UNITED STATES EMBASSY
LONDON, ENGLAND
1955

In Sydney, Saarinen was the judge of a fellow architect's work. But he evaluated his own projects no less rigorously. In the case of the United States Embassy in London, this reevaluation took the form of a stream of revisions to his original design.[15]

Saarinen's scheme for the embassy building, destined for the east side of Grosvenor Square, was selected in 1955 on the basis of a limited competition organized by the U.S. Department of State. The site had great symbolic significance for America: in 1785 a building at 9 Grosvenor Square housed John Adams, the first American minister to England; in 1913, 6 Grosvenor Square was the residence of the American ambassador; and in 1942, 20 Grosvenor Square was the general headquarters of the Allied Forces. The State Department guidelines were particularly mindful of the embassy's location, encouraging competitors "to grasp the historical meaning of the particular environment in which the new building must be set."[16]

The winning proposal, Saarinen knew, would have to further the tradition of quality in American federal architecture, as exemplified in Gordon Bunshaft's Bremen Consulate (1952), Edward Durell Stone's New Delhi Embassy (1954), and various projects conceived by the office of Foreign Buildings Operations. That Pietro Belluschi, a prominent modernist architect and dean of the MIT school of architecture, was a member of the competition jury boded well for a progressive design. The entries ranged from a conservative proposal by architect William Wurster to a highly experimental plan submitted by Minoru Yamasaki. Saarinen claimed first prize with a scheme that was at once modest, innovative, and controversial.[17]

Set back from the surrounding streets, the proposed building did not occupy the entire site. Saarinen had anticipated that the square would be completed in a pseudo-Georgian style; he therefore crafted a design that, though rather unusual, would reflect the neighboring buildings with "a uniform cornice line, red brick, Portland cement columns and balustrades." The plan is a testament to Saarinen's respect for federal architecture and the appropriateness of a certain classic style when designing public institutions. "I have no objection to the classic spirit," he remarked some years later. "For government buildings, such a spirit should prevail. But not the *style* or the *dilution* of the style. That is where the mistake is made."[18]

Saarinen took self-evaluation to an extreme in the London project. At each stage of design development the Saarinen office made numerous models and drawings, resulting in a series of facade drafts that provide a glimpse of how the architect evaluated his own work. Some of the drawings are fast sketches, done mostly in charcoal. Many of them depict the evolution of the west elevation, including close-ups of the final version. Two of Saarinen's freehand sketches show different concepts for the elevation, and a

ABOVE U.S. Embassy, London, 1955–60. © Wayne Andrews/Esto

further series of drawings elaborates on these two schemes. Building material and fenestration were the two main elements he used to achieve harmony with the other buildings around the square. "When the Portland stone on the new building darkens to the same tone as that on the surrounding edifices," he commented, the "continuity will be clearly seen." Saarinen also took note of the relationship between the windows, the existing facades, and their sculptural ornamentation. Experimenting with different scales and fenestration patterns, he tried out a host of solutions, pinning the various attempts up on a board, until he found the one that he considered most appropriate. Citing reflection as an essential element in his design, Saarinen's method might be described as design by choice. "Continual reevaluation is necessary. We must constantly question the validity of many of our practices," he said.[19]

The embassy stirred up a heated controversy. Architect Peter Smithson was especially critical of the way Saarinen's design embraced the Victorian period and accused Saarinen of taking the visual aspects of the building to the extreme without thinking about the nature of an embassy programmatically. "We are puzzled why you should want to emulate [the Victorian period], and should accept such frozen and pompous forms as the true expression of a generous egalitarian society," Smithson said. Critic Reyner Banham also condemned the building, chastising it as "monumental in bulk, frilly in detail." The objections expressed in England were probably well-founded, and Saarinen wasn't oblivious to them. He both declared the building "a complete success in the Grosvenor Square setting," and acknowledged his own hesitation. "In my own mind, the building is much better than the English think—but not quite as good as I wished it to be," he said a few years after its completion. Thus, he cast a critical eye over both the accusations and his own work. His ability to admit error—or the possibility of error—distanced him from the ideal of the aloof, infallible genius that captivated the architectural profession in the modern era. His characteristic doubt, and his willingness to reevaluate at all times, reflects his position as a member of the generation of designers who came of age after the modern movement's radical masters, who seemed to feel little need to question their own motives or designs.[20]

On the London embassy project, however, Saarinen's questioning was constant and thorough, and it recalled issues he frequently raised: "Have we gone overboard on the big windows, creating too many thermo-problems? Is the flat roof really the answer to all problems?"[21] Stretching testing to the limit was a recurring theme in Saarinen's practice, and often led him away from what was generally considered proper or tasteful. In his women's dormitories for the University of Pennsylvania (1957–60), he experimented with patterns of vertical and landscape windows, a playful design that also engaged in a more general questioning of some of the basic tenets of dormitory design. The same formal experimentation can be apprehended in the David S. Ingalls Hockey Rink at Yale University (1956–59), a work that in some places consciously toys with ugliness, or in the exaggerated shapes and proportions of the airport control tower at Dulles (1958–62).

The Sydney Opera House competition and the United States Embassy in London reflect two complementary aspects of Saarinen's activity as a critic. The insistence on reevaluation and "chasing the problem" are perhaps the most appealing traits Saarinen brought to competition judging and to the criticism of his own designs. In his desire to embrace everything, he considered every possible solution, and he was always open to experimentation, even at the risk of error or criticism.[22] These qualities make him especially attractive in light of the standards of architectural practice today.

EPILOGUE

In the end, you can only create and make
decisions according to your integrity.

For an architect of his stature, Saarinen did not publish much of his own writing. His original texts are scarce, and those that do exist are largely lecture transcripts. One notable exception is a full-length article he wrote for *Architectural Forum* in 1953. "The Six Broad Currents of Modern Architecture" examined a panoply of contemporary architects in order to show "each of the six forces" that Saarinen felt had "potency and meaning" for the architectural climate of his day.[1] Published when he was forty-two, this text is significant not just because it is a rare example of original writing by Saarinen, but because it identifies the diverse practitioners and practices that he saw as influential on his own work.

According to Saarinen, the six broad currents were: Frank Lloyd Wright's organic unity; the handicraft architecture of William Wurster and Pietro Belluschi; European individualism as exemplified by Alvar Aalto; Le Corbusier's functionalism and plastic form; Walter Gropius's machine-age architecture; and the form-giving vocabulary of Mies van der Rohe. In addition, Saarinen included the engineering-science of Pier Luigi Nervi and Buckminster Fuller. While he considered all of them "form-givers," as opposed to those who use form "inconsistently and indiscriminately, creating only confusion," he divided his icons into two main groups. On the one hand, individualists, romanticists, and humanists; on the other, classicists, functionalists, and practitioners of the International Style.[2]

In each category Saarinen saw various reciprocal influences among the constituents combining to form a kind of architectural ethos. For example, he noted that among the humanists, the spiritual quality in Wright's organic style could also be apprehended in the individualism of Wurster and Belluschi's craftwork, which, in turn, was related to the new romanticism of certain Northern European architects such as Aalto. Saarinen observed connections between the new dimensions in the architecture of Le Corbusier and the machine-age functionalism of Gropius and Mies, contrasting architectural forms inspired by painting and sculpture with the philosophy that inspired the Bauhaus. Further, he proposed that each of the six currents was subject to cross-pollination through interactions between architects. He found great hope in the way their fusion promised to respond to both the physical necessities and spiritual yearnings of contemporary culture:

> It is, therefore, logical to assume that, with the maturing of our civilization and the resulting respect for cultural, nonmaterialistic aims, spiritual qualities will flourish. They will catch up to the physical advances. Our architecture will then have the balance necessary for its flowering and some day will take an important place in history with the Greek, the Gothic and the Renaissance.[3]

Although the accuracy of Saarinen's classification is debatable and the optimism of his prognosis somewhat naïve, his analysis is a remarkable documentation of his wide-ranging interests and concerns. It is noteworthy that he made no reference to his father, the then-deceased Eliel Saarinen, since every one of the architectural strains described in the article was both practically and critically important to him, and he was certainly a prominent figure, especially among the Nordic group.

"Six Broad Currents" was not Saarinen's first public evaluation of his contemporaries. In 1958 he participated in author John Peter's series of interviews with sixteen modernist architects, later published as *The Oral History of Modern Architecture*. In the interview, Saarinen revealed his eclectic position by referring to the work of such luminaries as Wright, Le Corbusier, and Mies van der Rohe. With respect to Wright, Saarinen emphasized the American architect's principles over his forms. When it came to Corbusier, Saarinen admitted to feeling a special kinship to a fellow designer with a tendency to experiment in many realms. And regarding Mies, Saarinen remarked on a religious belief in structure, and on the Miesian characteristics in his own work, not only at the General Motors Technical Center, but also at the MIT auditorium. While acknowledging that Wright, Corbusier, and Mies represented the ABCs of modernism, Saarinen stated that "we have to broaden the alphabet of Modern Architecture."[4]

In another illuminating text, his 1954 address to the American Institute of Architects, Saarinen further developed his concept of an architectural ethos. This paper, "The Changing Philosophy of Architecture," described what Saarinen identified as the four key principles informing modernism's "rich and growing vocabulary." The first was architecture's need to express the Zeitgeist; the second, the importance of functional integrity; the third, that of structural integrity or clarity; and the fourth, the primacy of space versus mass. As a kind of "moral code," these four principles allowed for an "infinite number of expressions" within any architectural project, according to Saarinen. Additionally, Saarinen espoused a high regard for technology, texture and color, proportion, plastic form, historical architecture, contextual consideration, and outdoor space. Further passages in the paper referred to the need for constant reevaluation, something Saarinen repeated time and again in his lectures and commentaries. The "moral code"—and, thus, the potential for expressing spiritual values through architecture—was only rendered meaningful for Saarinen by the continual reevaluation of practice.[5]

In a lecture two years later at the Illinois Institute of Technology (IIT) campus, designed by Mies, on what makes architecture noble, Saarinen shifted his focus from "moral code" to "moral integrity":

Great architecture is both universal and individual. The individuality is achieved because the architecture is a true expression of its time. The individuality comes through—as at [IIT]—as a result of a special quality. It is a quality that is perhaps the least understood of all. It is a quality that cannot be taught. This quality is the philosophy and thinking behind architecture: is the expression of one man's unique combination of faith and honesty and devotion and beliefs in architecture, in short, his moral integrity.[6]

The emphasis on the individual, which was clearly reflected in Saarinen's practice as well as his discourse, is fundamentally modern, in so far as it projects an existential vision. In earlier periods—and even into the modern period, which had Le Corbusier's "Five Points"—well-defined architectural formulas were observed by academic design-ers. Saarinen, however, was finally guided by himself. "In the end, you can only create and make decisions according to your integrity," he said. Though difficult to pin down precisely, Saarinen's particular brand of integrity clearly involved absolute commitment to architecture, rigorous discipline, and the courage to constantly reevaluate one's own choices. (The Finnish word *sisu*, which connotes the strength that is born out of exhaus-tion, best captures his often agonizing manner of working.) Integrity for Saarinen meant a search for quality, and demanded a prioritization of the human spirit, a belief in techni-cal progress, a willingness to be expressive, a reverence for contextual propriety, and a deep understanding of the need for architecture to provide both physical comfort and emotional stimulation—all of which were recurrent themes in his work.[7]

Whether he was designing a chair, judging a competition, or researching traffic patterns for his next airport project, Saarinen's commitment to his principles was unflagging. For him, every project presented an opportunity for advancing in his quest to elevate humanity through architectural innovation. But in every case, that advance meant something different. Consequently, his body of work grew all the more eclectic and diverse as it developed. The right solution for a bank in Columbus, Indiana, had little in common with the right solution for a church in the same town, let alone a war memorial in Milwaukee or a rural college campus. In each case, Saarinen devised a unique design strategy. Thus, whereas the TWA Terminal was driven by his desire to convey the excitement of air travel, the plan for Yale University's residence halls grew out of a strikingly different interest in reinterpreting the contemplative community of a medieval cloister.

This is not to suggest that Saarinen only considered one design strategy per commission. Quite the opposite: In each case he examined a host of factors—client, site, program, budget, construction method, urban environment, aesthetic agenda, and so on—and then arranged them hierarchically before proceeding with a plan. In the CBS project, for example, his first concern was to reinvigorate the corporate image. Secondarily, he set his sights on advancing the language of mainstream office towers, given the city's new zoning ordinance. Of course, functional considerations always figured in the mix. Remarkably, Saarinen never succumbed to the temptation of adhering to a single template or style. His eclecticism was an eclecticism of procedure; his multiplicity a result of his multifaceted approach.

But turning each project into a unique example—a sort of exaggerated craft work—ran contrary to the architectural mass production so prevalent in postwar America. Saarinen was routinely accused of trying to reinvent the wheel. And some of his collaborators felt his professional manner lacked a clear sense of direction, because he routinely sounded out multiple options. Yet when necessary, Saarinen was willing to proceed methodically, carefully investigating functional precedents and proposing construction techniques that advertised his knowledge of state-of-the-art technique. His innovative bearing walls, mobile lounges, integrated air-conditioning systems, suspension-cable structures, and stressed-skin structures clearly advanced industrial production, yet each was devised in response to the unique needs of a singular project.

How did Saarinen's eclectic practice adapt itself so well to the production demands of a competitive architectural office? Carefully managed teamwork. "Unlike painting and sculpture, where the individual works entirely alone, architecture involves many people," Saarinen once remarked. "It is true that it all has to be siphoned through one mind, but there is always teamwork."[8] At its busiest, around 1956, the Bloomfield Hills office employed over sixty people, a relatively large staff, even by today's standards, for an American studio concentrating only on one-of-a-kind projects.

Given his unconventional, humanistic approach and his relentless attempt to broaden the modernist lexicon, Saarinen can rightly be seen as something of a postmodernist well before the advent of postmodernism. The term may be applied to Saarinen in much the same way it was first introduced by Joseph Hudnut, when he spoke of the postmodern house as belonging to a practice that succeeded the avant-gardes and the era of industrialization.[9] When Saarinen proposes multiple solutions to design problems, engages in self-reflective commentary about his own designs and those of his contemporaries, and explores meaning in a conscious manner that

foreshadows the escalating growth of communication in the postindustrial age, we can detect a sense of the postmodern condition in his practice.

Saarinen was ahead of his time in other respects, too. His distaste for architectural corporatization, for example, predates the concerns that plague the profession today. "Architecture has become too much of a business—a big business," he protested, and he unconditionally disparaged the architect-salesman, whose buildings were based solely on a "Kleenex-type" packaging, subservient only to the whims of fashion. Saarinen saw a tremendous need for a deeper commitment to architecture's humanistic promise: "Spirit, enthusiasm and dedication would finally make it fly," he asserted. He was always weary of mass production and consumption. The mounting sense of detachment in contemporary society—a by-product of mass-produced objects and uniform housing—could only be counterbalanced, in his view, by engaging environments that were designed with plenty of personality and were capable of conveying a sense of human identity. Saarinen's manifold quest might thus be summed up as an attempt to reconceive modernism in response to contemporary diversity, as a search for unity within a condition of plurality.

Is it possible to be guided by that ideal today, when modernity has so irreversibly imposed itself upon the paradigms of science, economics, and information? In response to this predicament, Saarinen offers us his work and inspiration, born out of a personal ethos of absolute commitment and faith in man.

ABOVE North Christian Church, Columbus, IN, 1959–63
RIGHT Concordia Senior College, Chapel, Fort Wayne, IN, 1954–58

INTRODUCTION

1. Vincent Scully, cited by Andrea O. Dean, "Eero Saarinen in Perspective," *AIA Journal* (November 1981): 36–51. Scully's criticism in Scully, *American Architecture and Urbanism* (New York: Henry Holt and Co., 1988), 198. Reference to shapes in Raymond Lifchez, "Eero Saarinen," *Zodiac* 17 (1967): 120–21; to bad taste in Gillo Dorfles, "Eero Saarinen: Recent Work," *Zodiac* 8: 85–89.

2. Aline Saarinen, general correspondence, AESP.

3. Henry-Russell Hitchcock, *Architecture: Nineteenth and Twentieth Centuries*, 4th ed. (New Haven: Yale University Press, 1977), 591.

4. J. M. Richards, *An Introduction to Modern Architecture*, 3rd ed. (Harmondsworth, England: Penguin Books, 1962), 112.

5. Peter Blake, *The Master Builders: Le Corbusier, Mies van der Rohe, Frank Lloyd Wright*, 3rd ed. (New York: Norton, 1996), 413.

6. Philip Johnson, letter of condolence to Aline Saarinen, n.d. [receipt by A.S., 8 September 1961], series IV, box 7, folder 70, ESP.

7. Among others, Bruce Adams, Charles Bassett, Robert Burley, Paul Kennon, Wilhem von Moltke, and Warren Platner also worked with Eero Saarinen.

8. Robert Venturi, interview by Tsukasa Yamashita, in Toshio Nakamura, ed., "Eero Saarinen," *A+U* (April 1984): 218–21.

9. Quoted in Aline Saarinen, ed., *Eero Saarinen on His Work* (New Haven: Yale University, 1962), 14 (October 1952).

10. Peter Carter, "Eero Saarinen, 1910–1961," *Architectural Design* (December 1961): 537.

11. Author's conversation with Kevin Roche, New Haven, Connecticut, 1997. Roche speaks in a similar sense in Dean, "Saarinen in Perspective."

12. Kevin Roche, interview by Yamashita, in Nakamura, ed., "Eero Saarinen," 20–24.

13. Eero Saarinen, April 1952, "Eero Saarinen—sketches, notes, correspondence," AESP 2.

14. *Bulletin of Yale University, School of Fine Arts*, New Haven, academic year 1931–32, Yjg 81 A2, 37–44, Manuscripts and Archives, Yale University.

15. See School of Fine Arts, box 13, folder 108; box 14, folders 126, 137, YRG.

16. There are no records of Eero Saarinen's academic works at either the Yale School of Architecture or Manuscripts and Archives, Yale University. His name appears in the lists of the *Bulletin* from years 1931–32 through 1933–34, and two of his works were published there: a police station in the subject Class B Design (*Bulletin* 1932–33, 49) and a water color subject (*Bulletin* 1932–33, 51).

They were also published in subsequent years. See *Bulletin of Yale University, School of Fine Arts* (New Haven: 1931, 1932, 1933) (Yjg 81 A2, Manuscripts and Archives, Yale University). David G. De Long tracked Eero Saarinen's academic works in his essay "Eliel Saarinen and the Cranbrook Tradition in Architecture and Urban Design," in Robert Judson Clark, *Design in America: The Cranbrook Vision, 1925–1950* (New York: Abrams; Detroit Institute of Arts; Metropolitan Museum of Art, 1983), 47–89, 296. Projects published and mentioned by De Long refer to the *Bulletin* of the Beaux Arts Institute of Design, and include: a police station, 1932; a synagogue, 1932; a city residence, 1933; an academy in Florence, 1933; a monument to J. S. Bach, 1933; a municipal market, 1933; a small courthouse, 1933; a new thousand-dollar bill, 1934; an industrial city, 1934; and a baroque fountain, 1934.

17. For a perspective on Cranbrook, see Clark, *Design in America*.

18. Other works by Eero Saarinen in collaboration with his father Eliel are: Berkshire Music Center, Massachusetts, 1938; Kleinhans Music Hall, Buffalo, New York, 1938–40; Wermuth House, Fort Wayne, Indiana, 1941–42; Summer Opera House, Lenox, Massachusetts, 1942, also with J. Robert Swanson; chapel in Stephens College, Columbia, Missouri, 1947; and the first project for General Motors Technical Center, Warren, Michigan, 1948–50.

19. Quoted in Saarinen, *Eero Saarinen*, 14 (26 April 1953).

20. Paul Heyer, *Architects on Architecture: New Directions in America* (New York: Walker, 1978), 286.

21. Advancing the line suggested by Heinrich Wölfflin, Meyer Shapiro wrote: "By style is meant the constant form—and sometimes the constant elements, qualities, and expression—in the art of an individual or society, as in speaking of 'life-style' or the 'style of a civilization.'" Shapiro, "Style," in A. L. Kroeber, ed., *Anthropology Today* (Chicago: University of Chicago Press, 1953), 287–312.

22. Quote by Frank Lloyd Wright, "In the Cause of Architecture II," *Architectural Record* (May 1914). "Les 'styles' sont un mensonge," Le Corbusier 1923, 67. "Form als Ziel is Formalismus; und den lehen wir ab. Ebensowenig erstreben wir einen Stil," Ludwig Mies van der Rohe, in "Bauen-Bauen," *G 2* (September 1923). Quote by Walter Gropius, in Gropius, *The New Architecture and the Bauhaus* (London: Faber & Faber, 1935; Cambridge, MA: MIT Press, 1965), 92.

23. Quoted in Saarinen, *Eero Saarinen*, 8 (18 April 1958).

24. "Great works of architecture, I thought, could only be created in a period such as those with a strong style sense, and that I could feel in the International Style of 1920–1930, a new and lasting 'Great Style' within which I would be glad to work." Philip

Johnson, *Writings* (New York: Oxford University Press, 1979), 247.

25. Hans-Georg Gadamer locates the origin of the use of the term *style* in French jurisprudence: "manière de procéder" or judicial procedure, and it has been employed in linguistics since the sixteenth century. See Gadamer, *Truth and Method* (New York: Seabury Press; Tübingen: J. C. B. Mohr, Paul Siebeck, 1975).

26. Statement written in Saarinen, *Eero Saarinen*, 36 (January 1959).

27. Reyner Banham was the first to formally link Saarinen with the phrase in his essay "The Fear of Eero's Mana," *Arts Magazine* (February 1962): 73. The phrase has also been associated with the term "functional eclecticism" proposed by Philip Johnson, "Informal Talk, Architectural Association, 1960," in Johnson, *Writings*, 104–16.

28. Charles Jencks refers to the adhocist designer, stating that "What he proposes is a lively and fumigated eclecticism." For Jencks, adhocism is the result of a fragmented totality. Jencks, "Adhocism," *Architectural Review* (July 1968): 27–30.

29. Diderot, quoted in Collins, *Changing Ideals in Modern Architecture, 1750–1950* (Montreal: McGill University Press, 1967), 17. Collins pursues "an architectural philosophy evolved in the spirit of true eclecticism," which he elaborates from Diderot.

30. Quoted in Saarinen, *Eero Saarinen*, 9 (1953).

31. When interviewed, Roche said that "Mies wanted to pull back all the layers and get to the heart. Eero wanted to embrace the entire body." Francesco Dal Co, *Kevin Roche* (New York: Rizzoli, 1985), 22.

32. Quoted in Saarinen, *Eero Saarinen*, 14 (29 January 1953).

CHAPTER 1 | CREATING

1. Saarinen, *Eero Saarinen*, 14 (22 July 1958).

2. J. P. Guilford, "Creativity," *The American Psychologist* (September 1950): 444–54. Later published in Guilford, *Intelligence, Creativity and Other Educational Implications* (San Diego: Robert R. Knapp, 1968), 77–96.

3. Donald W. MacKinnon, "The Nature and Nurture of Creative Talent," *The American Psychologist* (July 1962): 484–95. See also Alain Beaudot, *La créativité* (Paris: Bordas, 1973), 117–35.

4. Ibid. Refers to the mosaic test as designed by W. B. Hall and its conclusion.

5. Walter McQuade, "Eero Saarinen, A Complete Architect," *Architectural Forum* (April 1962): 104.

6. Saarinen, *Eero Saarinen*, 10 (1 December 1959).

7. MacKinnon, "The Nature and Nurture of Creative Talent," 490, 489; Saarinen, interview in *Horizon* (19 June 1959); Saarinen, *Eero Saarinen*, 8.

8. Saarinen, *Eero Saarinen*, 8, 4.

9. Saarinen, *Eero Saarinen*, 10 (30 April 1956).

10. April 1952, AESP 2; Saarinen, *Eero Saarinen*, 14.

11. Roche, conversation with the author.

12. Lawrence Lessing, "The Diversity of Eero Saarinen," *Architectural Forum* (July 1960): 95–6; Pelli, conversation with the author.

13. April 1952, AESP 2.

14. Isaiah Berlin, *The Hedgehog and the Fox* (New York: Simon & Schuster, 1953). Architectural scholar Colin Rowe discusses psychological types for architects based on Berlin's book. See also Rowe and Fred Koetter, *Collage City* (Cambridge, MA: MIT Press, 1978), 86; Saarinen, *Eero Saarinen*, 6 (22 July 1958).

15. "TWA's Graceful Air Terminal," *Architectural Forum* (January 1958): 78–85; Roche, conversation with the author.

16. Trans World Flight Center, TWA Buffet Program, 28 May 1962, series V, box 5, folder 9, SFP. Also published in Cranston Jones, *Architecture Today and Tomorrow* (New York: MacGraw-Hill Book Company, 1961), 145.

17. Quoted in series VII, box 13, folder 99, ESP. See also Saarinen, *Eero Saarinen*, 60.

18. Roche, conversation with the author.

19. Desk calendar, April 1957, series VII, box 11, folder 93, ESP. See also Peter Papademetriou, "TWA's Influence," *Progressive Architecture* (May 1992): 102–5.

20. "TWA's Graceful Air Terminal," 78–85. The models are also published in Allan Temko, *Eero Saarinen* (New York: George Braziller, 1962), fig. 95.

21. Christopher Hart Leubkeman, "Form Swallows Function," *Progressive Architecture* (May 1992): 106–9. Both Roche and Pelli refer to the grapefruit story in conversations with the author.

22. Pelli, conversation with the author; Roche, conversation with the author.

23. Carroll L. V. Meeks, *The Railroad Station, an Architectural History* (New Haven: Yale University Press, 1956), 138; Nikolaus Pevsner, *The Penguin Dictionary of Architecture* (London: Allen Lane, 1976), 232; Saarinen, *Eero Saarinen*, 60.

24. "TWA's Graceful Air Terminal," 81. Documenting the working model; there is an illustrated report of the working model by photographer Balthasar Korab, photographs from 1950s and 1960s, series II, box 4, folder 43, ESP; Saarinen, *Eero Saarinen*, 61; Gunnar Birkerts, interview by Yamashita, in Nakamura, ed., "Eero Saarinen," 223–25.

25. "TWA's Graceful Air Terminal." "[Eero] asked me to solve the problem of the building's legs. He designed them like perfect vertical columns. But when the engineers started calculating the shell cantilever, they concluded that the stress lines were like this [slanted], they crossed, and when the columns were made like that they looked terrible. Then [Eero] asked me to solve the problem[....]The problem was complex because each one of these stress lines had an amplitude of movement, given the changes of wind and snow, the stress could come from here or there. The engineers gave me the minimal sections and, based on that, I modeled a series of wire, and I shaped the legs." Pelli, conversation with the author.

26. The number of plans corresponding to project I is 568, Trans World Airlines, Kennedy Airport, No. 5603, ESA; "Shaping a Two-Acre Sculpture," *Architectural Forum* (August 1960): 118–23. Framework.

27. "TWA's Graceful Air Terminal," 78–85; "Shaping a Two-Acre Sculpture," 118–23; "The Concrete Bird Stands Free," *Architectural Forum* (December 1960): 114–5; "Idlewild, New York International Airport," *Architectural Record* (September 1961): 162–64; Scully, *American Architecture and Urbanism*, 198.

28. Temko, *Eero Saarinen*, 48.
29. Thomas Fisher, "Landmarks: TWA Terminal,"*Progressive Architecture* (May 1992): 96–101; Reyner Banham, *Age of the Masters: A Personal View of Modern Architecture* (London: Architectural Press, 1975), 125. See also Banham, "The Obsolescent Airport," *Architectural Review* (October 1962): 252–53.
30. "Shaping a Two-Acre Sculpture,"118–23.
31. "The Concrete Bird Stands Free," 114; "TWA's Graceful Air Terminal," 79; Temko, *Eero Saarinen*, 47; Zevi, *Storia dell'architettura moderna* (Torino: Giulio Einaudi, 1975), 383; Saarinen, *Eero Saarinen*, 60; Statement of the Trans World Airlines at Idlewild, New York, series VII, box 13, folder 99, ESP.
32. Temko, *Eero Saarinen*, 47; Saarinen, *Eero Saarinen*, 8; Robert Venturi, interview by Yamashita, Nakamura, ed., "Eero Saarinen," 219.
33. Zevi, *Storia dell'architettura moderna*, 379; Françoise Fichet, *La théorie architecturale a l'age classique* (Brussels: Pierre Mardaga, 1979), 38. Fichet takes the expression "architecture active" from A. Wogensky. See also Étienne-Louis Boullée, *Architecture, essai sur l'art* (Paris: Hermann, 1968), 48–9.
34. Saarinen, *Eero Saarinen*, 6 (1 December 1959). See also series VII, box 13, folder 97, ESP.
35. Saarinen, interview in *Horizon* (July 1960): 76–82, 122–3; Saarinen, *Eero Saarinen*, 6; Hitchcock, *Architecture*, 590–91.

CHAPTER 2 | DWELLING

1. Martin Heidegger, *The Question Concerning Technology and Other Essays* (New York: Harper & Row, 1977), 143–61.
2. Dal Co, *Kevin Roche*, 23.
3. Ibid.
4. Beatriz Colomina, "Reflections on the Eames House," in Donald Albrecht, ed., *The Work of Charles and Ray Eames: A Legacy of Invention* (New York: Abrams, 1997), 127–49.
5. John Peter, *The Oral History of Modern Architecture: Interviews with the Greatest Architects of the Twentieth Century* (New York: Abrams, 1994), 206–7. Statement from 1958.
6. Ibid, 88.
7. Note by Steve Kerezian, director of Yale University News Bureau, 23 September 1962, box 213, folder 1965, YRG; Letter from Paul Mellon to president Griswold, 3 June 1958, box 213, folder 1961, YRG; Note by Kerezian, 8 June 1958, box 213, folder 1961, YRG; Note by Kerezian, 7 April 1959, box 213, folder 1963, YRG.
8. *Yale News*, 12 November 1959. Description of the budget; Saarinen shows his concern with keeping to the budget, letter from Saarinen to A. Whitney Griswold, 26 May 1959, box 213, folder 1962, YRG; A. Whitney Griswold, "A Proposal for Strengthening the Residential College System in Yale University," 29 April 1958, box 285, folder 2520, YRG.
9. Statement by Saarinen on the colleges, 4 November 1959, series VII, box 13, folder 99, ESP. Also published in Saarinen, *Eero Saarinen*, 80.
10. Ibid.; *Yale News*, 1. References to rooms and budget details; box 213, folder 1962, YRG.
11. Eero Saarinen, "The Changing Philosophy of Architecture," *Architectural Record* (August 1954): 182; Colin Rowe and Fred Koetter, "The Crisis of the Object: The Predicament of Texture," *Perspecta* 16 (1980): 109–42. The two models are proposed as the spirit of place and the spirit of time.
12. The effect of integration and passage has been altered in Morse College, where other groups of sculptures have been placed. Such is the case with *Lipstick* by Claes Oldenburg, which relegates Costantino Nivola's sculptures to the background.
13. Saarinen, *Eero Saarinen*, 68.
14. Eliot F. Noyes, *Organic Design in Home Furnishings*. The detail of series, finishing, and manufacturing; John Neuhart, Marilyn Neuhart, and Ray Eames, *Eames Design: the Work of the Office of Charles and Ray Eames* (New York: Abrams, 1989), 25. Refers to the furniture competition. See also R. Craig Miller, "Interior Design Furniture," in Clark, *Design in America*, 91–143, or Eric Larrabee, *Knoll Design* (New York: Abrams, 1981), 12–17, 50–65.
15. Saarinen, *Eero Saarinen*, 11 (19 June 1958).
16. Joseph Giovannini, "The Office of Charles Eames and Ray Kaiser: The Material Trail," in Albrecht, *The Work of Charles and Ray Eames*, 45–71. Interview with Don Albison; Neuhart, Neuhart, and Eames, *Eames Design*, 25; Pat Kirkham, *Charles and Ray Eames: Designers of the Twentieth Century* (Cambridge, MA: MIT Press, 1995), 210.
17. Saarinen, *Eero Saarinen*, 68; Letter 14 July 1949, series IV, box 8, folder 80, ESP.
18. Saarinen, *Eero Saarinen*, 68.
19. Patent 2,541,835 United States Patent Office, series VIII, box 14, folder 7, ESP; Donald Miller, *The Lewis Mumford Reader* (New York: Pantheon Books, 1986), 120. Miller takes dates from Christine Rae, ed., *Knoll au Louvre* (New York: 1971).
20. Saarinen, *Eero Saarinen*, 68.
21. Constructive drawings for the Pedestal Chair, "Eero Saarinen Furniture," ESA; Affiche Knoll, series VI, box 6, folder 62, ESP.
22. Affiche Knoll, series VI, box 6, folder 62, ESP.
23. Saarinen, address 24 October 1960, "Schoner Wohnen" Congress, Munich, Germany, series VII, box 13, folder 97, ESP.

CHAPTER 3 | BUILDING

1. María Moliner, *Diccionario de uso del Español* (Madrid: Gredos, 1966).
2. Ibid., 4; Antoine Picon, *L'art de l'ingenieur* (Paris: Centre Georges Pompidou, 1997). The catalog on the exhibition on engineering staged in 1997 at the Centre Pompidou, Paris, highlights Saarinen, one of the few architects included in the exhibition.
3. "Saarinen," *Architectural Forum* (September 1961): 113.
4. Series VII, box 13, folder 98, ESP. See also Saarinen, *Eero Saarinen*, 92.
5. Norman Bel Geddes, *Horizons* (Boston: Little, Brown, and Company, 1932), 79–121.
6. Saarinen's statement on the terminal building of Dulles International Airport, series VII, box 13, folder 98, ESP. See also Saarinen, *Eero Saarinen*, 92–96.
7. Temko, *Eero Saarinen*, 115 (editor's insertion).

8. Neuhart, Neuhart, and Eames, *Eames Design*, 231.

9. "Passenger Terminal Buildings Design Principles," *Architectural Record* (March 1960): 167–82.

10. Series VII, box 13, folder 98, ESP. See also Saarinen, *Eero Saarinen*, 92–96; "Passenger Terminal Buildings Design Principles," 167–82; Series VII, box 13, folder 98, ESP.

11. Series II, box 2, folder 25, ESP.

12. "Yale's Viking Vessel," *Architectural Forum* (December 1958): 106–11; "Music Tent," *Architectural Forum* (September 1949): 88–89.

13. Mario Salvadori, *Why Buildings Stand Up: The Strength of Architecture* (New York: Norton, 1980), 264–65; "Building Engineering," *Architectural Forum* (June 1953): 168–73.

14. For budgets and program, see "FAA Announces Design of Terminal Building for Dulles International Airport," 31 January 1960, CA. See also "Saarinen," 113.

15. Temko, *Eero Saarinen*, 114.

16. Ibid.

17. Series VII, box 13, folder 98, ESP. See also Saarinen, *Eero Saarinen*, 96.

18. "A Compendium of Relative Facts to Date," 15 July 1949, box 1, folder "1949," JNEMA Records (series V, box 5, folder 13, JNEM, SFP, CA); The different plans are accounted for in "Dedication of the Gateway Arch Program" (Saint Louis, MO: 1968), series III, box 5, folder 57, ESP.

19. The program of the competition corresponds to Architectural Competition for the National Expansion Memorial Program (Saint Louis, MO: 1947), folder "JNEM 361," Vertical File, JNEM Library, JNEM Archives (series V, box 5, folder 15, JNEM, SFP, CA).

20. "Competition, Jefferson National Expansion Memorial," *Progressive Architecture* (May 1948): 51–71. See also "Jefferson National Expansion Memorial Competition," *Architectural Forum* (March 1948): 14–18.

21. The plan of the final proposal was published in *Progressive Architecture* and *Architectural Forum*. See also series II, box 2, folder 5, ESP; Saarinen's text describing the visit corresponds to "A Tour Through the Jefferson National Expansion Memorial," box 5, folder "Tour of Proposed JNEM, Saarinen 1948," JNEMA Records (JNEM, CA).

22. Competition Drawings, box 4, folder "1947 Memorial Competition Entry Drawings," JNEMA Records (JNEM, CA). "Summary of Comments of Jury of Award on Winning Designs."

23. George McCue, "The Arch: An Appreciation," *AIA Journal* 67 (November 1978): 57–63; In June 1960 the sum of $2,953,000 was appropriated by Congress for the Jefferson National Expansion Memorial, allowing the project to continue. "Annual Report of Morton D. May," 7 June 1961, box 1, folder "1961," JNEMA Records (series V, box 5, folder 13, JNEM, SFP, CA); McCue, "The Arch: An Appreciation," 61.

24. Quoted in Papademetriou "Severud (Fred N.)" in Picon, *L'art de l'ingenieur*, 453–55; Carl W. Condit, *American Building*, 2nd ed. (Chicago: University of Chicago, 1982), 206. Other engineers who contributed to the structure were Perrone, Fischer, Conlin, and Bandel, of New York.

25. A detailed description is in "Dedication of the Gateway Arch: Jefferson National Expansion Memorial, Saint Louis, Missouri, 25 May 1968, Program," series III, box 5, folder 57, ESP.

26. Condit, *American Building*, 207.

27. "Competition, Jefferson National Expansion Memorial," 58; Mike Capps, et al., *Story of the Gateway Arch* (Saint Louis: Jefferson National Expansion Historical Association, 1992), 12–14.

28. Saarinen's statement "Jefferson National Expansion Park, Saint Louis, Missouri," January 1959, series VIII, box 13, folder 99, ESP. See also Saarinen, *Eero Saarinen*, 18.

29. After the jury decision, on 17 February 1948, letter from Gilmore D. Clarke to William W. Wurster, dated 24 February 1948, box 5, folder "Libera vs. Saarinen," JNEMA Records (JNEM, CA); Gabriella Belli, et al., *Adalberto Libera: Opera Completa* (Milan: Electa, 1989), 162–63. See also Francesco Garofalo and Luca Veresani, *Adalberto Libera* (Bologna: Zanichelli, 1989), 107–9.

30. Letter from Hugh Ferriss to Luther Ely Smith, 1 March 1948, box 5, folder "Libera vs. Saarinen," JNEM Records (JNEM, CA); Lawyers Sereni & Herzfeld of New York, representing Libera, propose Saarinen a settlement. Letter from Angelo Piero Sereni to Saarinen, 24 June 1948, box 5, folder "Libera vs. Saarinen," JNEMA Records (JNEM, CA); *New York Herald Tribune*, 26 Feb 1948, box 5, folder "Architectural Controversy Over Arch Design," JNEMA Records (JNEM, CA); In a memorandum addressed to Mrs. Forthmann, 18 March 1948, William W. Wurster encloses the statement of the jury in response to Gilmore D. Clarke. The quotation is in "Statement by the Jury of Award on the Winning Design in the Jefferson National Expansion Memorial Competition," box 5, folder "Libera vs. Saarinen," JNEMA Records (JNEM, CA).

31. Saarinen, *Eero Saarinen*, 18. See also "Jefferson National Expansion Park, Saint Louis, Missouri," series VIII, box 13, folder 99, ESP.

CHAPTER 4 | SOCIALIZING

1. Lewis Mumford, *The Culture of Cities* (New York: Harcourt Brace & Company, 1970), 5.

2. Series VII, box 13, folder 97, ESP. See also Saarinen, *Eero Saarinen*, 6 (1 December 1959).

3. Saarinen, *Eero Saarinen*, 8 (16 June 1954).

4. Eliel Saarinen, *The City: Its Growth, Its Decay, Its Future* (New York: Reinhold Publishing Corporation, 1943), 216–17.

5. Arthur M. Schlesinger, *The Cycles of American History* (Boston: Houghton Mifflin, 1986), 32.

6. Temko, *Eero Saarinen*, 20.

7. Charles F. Kettering, "Tomorrow's Challenge," *General Motors Technical Center*, brochure. By 1947 the younger Saarinen's involvement in the project was already evident in the altered forms of certain structures, such as the Miesian Dynamometer Building.

8. Statement "General Motors Technical Center," series VII, box 13, folder 98, ESP.

9. Ibid.

10. *General Motors Technical Center*, brochure. See also Albert Christ-Janer, *Eliel Saarinen*, 2nd ed. (Chicago: University of Chicago Press, 1979), 126–28.

11. The statement "Summary of the Architecture of the General

Motors Technical Center" mentions Versailles when addressing the fountain system, series VII, box 13, folder 98, ESP; "GM's Industrial Versailles," *Architectural Forum* (May 1956): 122–30. Nevertheless, it is probable that neither this summary nor any one of the complex statements was personally written by Saarinen.

12. "General Motors Technical Center."

13. Alan Colquhoun, *Essays in Architectural Criticism: Modern Architecture and Historical Change* (Cambridge, MA: MIT Press, 1981), 83–103.

14. "Summary of the Architecture of General Motors Technical Center," 6.

15. "General Motors Technical Center."

16. "Summary of the Architecture of General Motors Technical Center," 12–13.

17. Plan of lobby furniture, administration building, research staff group, "General Motors," ESA; The lobby is described in the text "Architectural Notes on the Research Staff Building of the General Motors Technical Center," series VII, box 13, folder 98, ESP.

18. "Summary of the Architecture of General Motors Technical Center."

19. "General Motors Technical Center," *Architectural Forum* (November 1951): 111–23; Roche, conversation with the author; "General Motors," ESA.

20. See "Summary of the Architecture of General Motors Technical Center."

21. "Summary of the Architecture of General Motors Technical Center." There is also a good description of the panels in "GM Nears Completion," *Architectural Forum* (November 1954).

22. Daniel Bell, *The Coming of Post-Industrial Society* (New York: Basic Books, 1973), 20.

23. Robert A. M. Stern, Thomas Mellins, and David Fishman, *New York 1960* (New York: Monacelli Press), 406–10; for a complete review of the building, see "CBS Skyscraper Plan Announced," series VII, box 13, folder 98, ESP.

24. The ground-floor drawing corresponds to the sketch series, folio II, folder 10, ESP.

25. "New York Rethinks Its City Plan," *Architectural Forum* (September 1950): 124; Kenneth Halpern, *Downtown USA: Urban Design in Nine American Cities* (New York: Watson-Guptill Publications, 1978), 23.

26. Roche, conversation with the author.

27. Saarinen, *Eero Saarinen*, 16.

28. Roche, conversation with the author.

29. Quoted in Saarinen, *Eero Saarinen*, 16 (1961).

30. Roche, conversation with the author. "[He] was interested in doing the first concrete high-rise in New York...."

31. "Saarinen's Skyscraper," *Architectural Record* (July 1965): 113–18.

32. "Columbia Broadcasting System Headquarters" (New York: CBS, 1964), series III, box 6, folder 62, ESP.

33. "Saarinen's Skyscraper," 113. See also Stern, Mellins, and Fishman, *New York 1960*, 408.

34. Saarinen, *Eero Saarinen*, 16; statement to a client, 31 March 1961.

35. "Distinguished Interior Architecture for CBS," *Architectural Record* (June 1966): 129–34; "Design at CBS," *Industrial Design* (February 1966). Patricia Conway notes the preponderance of straight-line compositions arranged to complement the furniture; Stern, Mellins, and Fishman, *New York 1960*, 409.

CHAPTER 5 | JUDGING

1. Robert Venturi, *Complexity and Contradiction in Architecture*, 2nd ed. (New York: Museum of Modern Architecture, 1977), 13.

2. Roche, conversation with the author. "[Eero] wanted to win, always win; in a meeting like the [Sydney] competition he wanted to pick the winner."

3. McQuade, "Eero Saarinen"; Venturi, *Complexity and Contradiction*, 13.

4. Philip Drew, *Sydney Opera House* (London: Phaidon, 1995), 6–7.

5. "Assessors' Report" (text sent to competitors by R. J. Thomson, Secretary and Executive Officer, Opera House Committee, Department of Local Government, Public Works Building, Cr. Philip and Bridge Streets, Sydney, Australia); courtesy of Philip Drew. An edited version is published in "A New Personality: Jørn Utzon," *Zodiac* 5 (1959): 99.

6. "Assessors' Report."

7. Sigfried Giedion, "Jørn Utzon and the Third Generation: A New Chapter of 'Space, Time and Architecture,'" *Zodiac* 14 (1965): 36–47.

8. Hilde De Haan and Ids Haagsma, *Architects in Competition* (London: Thames and Hudson, 1988), 136–45; ibid., 140–41.

9. Series II, box 3, folder 31, ESP. Photographs of the two drawings are classified within the documents for the article McQuade, "Eero Saarinen," although they are not published there.

10. Peter Collins, *Architectural Judgement* (London: Faber & Faber, 1971), 44–45; "Assessors' Report"; Saarinen, *Eero Saarinen*, 10 (2 June 1957).

11. Desk calendar, April 1957, series VII, box 11, folder 93, ESP; "Assessors' Report."

12. "Assessors' Report"; Philip Drew, *Third Generation: The Changing Meaning of Architecture* (London: Pall Mall Press, 1972); Giedion, "Jørn Utzon and the Third Generation."

13. Félix Candela, "El escándalo de la Ópera de Sidney," *Arquitectura* (December 1967): 29–34. See also Félix Candela, *En defensa del formalismo y otros escritos* (Madrid: Xarait, 1985), 57–64. As a response to Candela, see Rafael Moneo, "Sobre el Escandalo de Sidney," *Arquitectura* (January 1968): 52–54.

14. "Assessors' Report."

15. Series VII, box 13, folder 97, ESP. "Therefore, continual reevaluation is necessary," in Saarinen, "The Changing Philosophy of Architecture." Speech at the eighty-sixth convention of the AIA, Boston, MA, in June 1954. See also *Architectural Forum* (August 1954): 182.

16. Fello Atkinson, "U.S. Building, Grosvenor Square, London," *Architectural Review* (April 1961): 252–62. Collection of the competition particularities.

17. "U.S. Architecture Abroad," *Architectural Forum* (March 1953): 101–15. A reference to related buildings in progress within the

Department of State at the time. "Architecture to Represent America Abroad," *Architectural Record* (May 1955): 187–92; Atkinson, "U.S. Building, Grosvenor Square, London," 252–62.

18. Series VII, box 13, folder 99, ESP. See also Saarinen, *Eero Saarinen*, 8, 48.

19. Series II, box 2, folders 14, 15, ESP; Series VII, box 13, folder 99, ESP; Series VII, box 13, folder 99, ESP. "This wall structure of coupled precast concrete columns alternately placed above each other creates a fenestration that is related to that of the other buildings as well as giving us the desired plastic quality," Saarinen stated; Saarinen, "The Changing Philosophy of Architecture," 182.

20. "Controversial Building in London," *Architectural Forum* (March 1961): 80–85; Saarinen, *Eero Saarinen*, 35–36, 48. Saarinen also expressed such self-criticism when it came to other build-ings. Remarking on the MIT auditorium, he allowed: "The exte-rior of the [MIT] auditorium has generated a good deal of dis-cussion, pro and con. I think some of the criticisms have a cer-tain amount of justification. I feel now that the building is not enough of a lifting form and that perhaps it does lack sufficient definition of scale."

21. Saarinen, "The Changing Philosophy of Architecture," 182.

22. Pelli, conversation with the author. Highlighting Saarinen's explo-ration, Pelli refers to some projects the latter considered as failed: Concordia Senior College, Fort Wayne, Indiana, 1953–58, and the Women's Dormitory at the University of Chicago, Illinois, 1955–58.

EPILOGUE

1. Eero Saarinen, "The Six Broad Currents of Modern Architecture," *Architectural Forum* (July 1953): 110–15.

2. Ibid.

3. Ibid.

4. Peter, *The Oral History of Modern Architecture*.

5. Saarinen, "The Changing Philosophy of Architecture." Addresses by Paul Rudolph, José Luis Sert, Saarinen, William W. Wurster, and Ralph Walker; Saarinen, "The Changing Philosophy of Architecture."

6. Saarinen, *Eero Saarinen*, 10 (30 April 1956).

7. Saarinen, *Eero Saarinen*, 14; Temko, *Eero Saarinen*, 14. Notes how Saarinen translated *sisu* as "extended guts."

8. Saarinen, *Eero Saarinen*, 10 (1 December 1959).

9. Joseph Hudnut, "The Post-Modern House," *Architectural Review* (May 1945): 70–75.

ARCHIVES

Eero Saarinen Papers [ESP]. Manuscript group number 593, Manuscripts and Archives, Yale University.

A. Whitney Griswold. *Presidential Records*. [YRG] 2A16, Manuscripts and Archives, Yale University. Also *School of Fine Arts 1869–1955 (defunct)*, 1832–1969, YRG-16E.

Saarinen Collection. Drawings and watercolors annex to the collection *Eero Saarinen Papers* [ESP]. Yale Art Gallery, Yale University.

Saarinen Family Papers [SFP]. Acquisition number 1990–08, Cranbrook Archives, Cranbrook Educational Community.

Mark Coir Files. Cranbrook Archives [CA], Cranbrook Educational Community.

Aline and Eero Saarinen Papers [AESP]. Archives of American Art, Smithsonian Institution.

Jefferson National Expansion Memorial Association [JNEMA] *Records*. Accession JEFF-985, Jefferson National Expansion Memorial [JNEM] Archives, National Park Service.

Eero Saarinen Archives [ESA]. Roche & Dinkeloo, Hamden, Connecticut.

BOOKS

Abalos, Iñaki, and Juan Herreros. *Técnica y arquitectura en la ciudad contemporánea*. Madrid: Nerea, 1992.

Albrecht, Donald, et al. *The Work of Charles and Ray Eames: A Legacy of Invention*. New York: Abrams, 1997.

Alexander, Christopher. *Notes on the Synthesis of Form*. Cambridge, MA: Harvard University Press, 1964.

Augustyn, Robert T., and Paul E. Cohen. *Manhattan in Maps, 1527–1995*. New York: Rizzoli, 1997.

Banham, Mary, et al., eds. *A Critic Writes: Essays by Reyner Banham*. Berkeley: University of California Press, 1996.

Banham, Reyner. *Age of the Masters: A Personal View of Modern Architecture*. London: Architectural Press, 1975.

———. *The Architecture of the Well-Tempered Environment*. London and Chicago: Architectural Press and University of Chicago Press, 1969.

———. *Design by Choice*. London: Academy Editions, 1981.

Bell, Daniel. *The Coming of Post-Industrial Society*. New York: Basic Books, 1973.

Belli, Gabriella, et al. *Adalberto Libera. Opera completa*. Milan: Electa, 1989.

Blake, Peter. *The Master Builders: Le Corbusier, Mies van der Rohe, Frank Lloyd Wright*. 3d ed. New York: Norton, 1996.

Boullée, Étienne-Louis. *Architecture, essai sur l'art*. Reprint. Paris: Hermann, 1968.

Bourdieu, Pierre. *La distinction: critique sociale du jugement*. Paris: Les Éditions de Minuit, 1979.

Bulletin of Yale University. New Haven: Yale School of Fine Arts, 1931–33.

Calvino, Italo. *Six Memos for the Next Millennium*. Cambridge, MA: Harvard University Press, 1988.

Cantacuzino, Sherban. "Eero Saarinen." In *Great Modern Architecture*. London: Studio Vista, 1966.

Capps, Mike, et al. *Story of the Gateway Arch*. Saint Louis: Jefferson National Expansion Historical Association, 1992.

Christ-Janer, Albert. *Eliel Saarinen*. 2d ed. Chicago: University of Chicago Press, 1979.

Ciucci, Giorgio, Francesco Dal Co, Mario Manieri Elia, and Manfredo Tafuri. *La città americana della guerra civile al New Deal*. Roma-Bari: Casa Editrice Gius; Laterza & Figli, 1973.

Clark, Robert Judson. *Design in America: The Cranbrook Vision, 1925–1950*. New York: Abrams; Detroit Institute of Arts; Metropolitan Museum of Art, 1983.

Collins, Peter. *Architectural Judgement*. London: Faber & Faber, 1971.

———. *Changing Ideals in Modern Architecture 1750–1950*. Montreal: McGill University Press, 1967.

Colquhoun, Alan. *Essays in Architectural Criticism: Modern Architecture and Historical Change*. Cambridge, MA: MIT Press, 1981.

Condit, Carl W. *American Building*. 2d ed. Chicago: University of Chicago, 1982.

Dal Co, Francesco. *Kevin Roche*. New York: Rizzoli, 1985.

De Haan, Hilde, and Ids Haagsma. *Architects in Competition*. London: Thames and Hudson, 1988.

Department of City Planning. *Zoning Handbook: A Guide to New York City's Zoning Resolution*. New York: Department of City Planning, 1990.

Drew, Philip. *Sydney Opera House*. London: Phaidon, 1995.

———. *Third Generation: The Changing Meaning of Architecture*. London: Pall Mall Press, 1972.

Drexler, Arthur, ed. *The Architecture of the École des Beaux-Arts*. London: Secker & Warburg; New York: Museum of Modern Art, 1977.

Ferriss, Hugh. *The Metropolis of Tomorrow*. New York: Ives Washburn, 1929. Reprint. New York: Princeton Architectural Press, 1986.

Fichet, Françoise. *La théorie architecturale à l'âge classique*. Brussels: Pierre Mardaga, 1979.

Foucault, Michel. *L'Hermenéutique du sujet*. Paris: Gallimard, Le Seuil, 2001.

————. *Les mots et les choses. Une archéologie des sciences humaines*. Paris: Gallimard, 1966.

Frampton, Kenneth. *Studies in Tectonic Culture*. Cambridge, MA: MIT Press, 1995.

Gadamer, Hans Georg. *Truth and Method*. New York: Seabury Press; Tübingen: J. C. B. Mohr, Paul Siebeck, 1975.

Garofalo, Francesco, and Luca Verasani. *Adalberto Libera*. Bologna: Zanichelli, 1989.

Gavinelli, Corrado. *Eero Saarinen. Il terminal dell'aeroporto internazionale Dulles*. Kyoto: Dososha Shuppan, 1984. Reprint. Milan: Jaca Books, 1994.

Geddes, Norman Bel. *Horizons*. Boston: Little, Brown, and Company, 1932. Reprint. New York: Dover, 1977.

Giedion, Sigfried. *Space, Time and Architecture*. 5th ed. Cambridge, MA: Harvard University Press, 1982.

Gropius, Walter. *The New Architecture and the Bauhaus*. London: Faber & Faber, 1935; Cambridge, MA: MIT Press, 1965.

Guilford, J. P. *Intelligence, Creativity and Other Educational Implications*. San Diego: Robert R. Knapp, 1968.

Guiraud, Pierre. *La stylistique*. Paris: Presses Universitaires de France, 1967.

Hall, Mildred Reed, and Edward T. Hall. *The Fourth Dimension in Architecture: The Impact of Building on Behavior. Eero Saarinen's Administrative Center for Deere & Company, Moline, Illinois*. Santa Fe: Sunstone Press, 1975.

Halpern, Kenneth. *Downtown USA. Urban Design in Nine American Cities*. New York: Watson-Guptill Publications, 1978.

Hausen, Marika, et al. *Eliel Saarinen: Projects, 1896–1923*. Hamburg: Gingko Press, 1990.

Heidegger, Martin. *Poetry, Language, Thought*. New York: Harper & Row, 1971.

————. *The Question Concerning Technology and Other Essays*. New York: Harper & Row, 1977.

Heyer, Paul. *Architects on Architecture: New Directions in America*. New York: Walker, 1978.

Hitchcock, Henry-Russell. *Architecture: Nineteenth and Twentieth Centuries*. 4th ed. New Haven: Yale University Press, 1977.

Hozumi, Nobuo. GA 26, *Eero Saarinen: TWA Terminal Building, Dulles International Airport*. Photographs by Yukio Futagawa. Tokyo: Ada Edita, 1973.

Iglesia, E. J. *Eero Saarinen*. Buenos Aires: Instituto de Arte Americano e Investigaciones Estéticas, 1966.

Jacobs, Jane. *The Death and Life of Great American Cities*. New York: Random House, 1961.

James, William. "Pragmatism: A New Name for Some Old Ways of Thinking." In *Pragmatism and the Meaning of Truth*. Cambridge, MA. Harvard University Press, 1978.

Jefferson, Thomas. *Writings*. New York: Literary Classics of the United States, 1984.

Johnson, Philip. *Mies van der Rohe*. New York: Museum of Modern Art, 1947.

————. *Writings*. New York: Oxford University Press, 1979.

Jones, Cranston. *Architecture Today and Tomorrow*. New York: MacGraw-Hill Book Company, 1961.

Jordy, William H. *American Buildings and Their Architects, Vol. 5. The Impact of European Modernism in the Mid-Twentieth Century*. New York: Oxford University Press, 1972.

Kaufmann, Emil. *Three Revolutionary Architects: Boullée, Ledoux, and Lequeu*. Philadelphia: American Philosophical Society, 1952.

Kirkham, Pat. *Charles and Ray Eames: Designers of the Twentieth Century*. Cambridge, MA: MIT Press, 1995.

Koolhaas, Rem, and Bruce Mau. *S, M, L, XL*. New York: Monacelli Press, 1995.

Krauss, Rosalind E. *Richard Serra/Sculpture*. New York: Museum of Modern Art, 1986.

Kruft, Hanno-Walter. *A History of Architectural Theory from Vitruvius to the Present*. New York: Princeton Architectural Press, 1994.

Lang, Berel. *The Concept of Style*. 2d ed. Ithaca: Cornell University Press, 1987.

Larrabee, Eric. *Knoll Design*. New York: Abrams, 1981.

Le Corbusier. *La charte d'Athènes*. Paris: Éditions de Minuit, 1957.

————. *Précisions sur un état présent de l'architecture et l'urbanisme*. Paris: Crès et Cie, 1930. Reprint. Paris: Altamira, 1994.

————. *Vers une architecture*. Paris: Crès et Cie, 1923. Reprint. Paris: Arthaud, 1977; Cambridge, England: Cambridge University Press, 1989.

Madec, Philippe. *Boullée*. Paris: Fernand Hazan, 1986.

Mallgrave, Henry Francis, and Wolfgang Herrmann. *Gottfried Semper: The Four Elements of Architecture [1851] and Other Writings*. Cambridge, MA: MIT Press, 1984.

Meeks, Carroll L. V. *The Railroad Station: An Architectural History*. New Haven: Yale University Press, 1956.

Merleau-Ponty, Maurice. *La structure du comportement*. 4th ed. Paris: Presses Universitaires de France, 1960.

Mújica, Francisco. *History of the Skyscraper*. Paris: Archaeology and Architecture Press, 1929.

Mumford, Lewis. *The Culture of Cities*. New York: Harcourt Brace & Company, 1970.

Neuhart, John, Marilyn Neuhart, and Ray Eames. *Eames Design: The Work of the Office of Charles and Ray Eames*. New York: Abrams, 1989.

Norberg-Schulz, Christian. *Scandinavia*. Milan: Electa, 1990.

Noyes, Eliot F. *Organic Design in Home Furnishings*. New York: Museum of Modern Art, 1941.

Pelli, Cesar, and Diana Pelli. GA 6. *Eero Saarinen: Bell Telephone Corporation Research Laboratories, New Jersey, 1957–63; Deere & Company Headquarters Building, Illinois, 1957–63*. Photographs by Yukio Futagawa. Tokyo: Ada Edita, 1971.

Peter, John. *The Oral History of Modern Architecture: Interviews with the Greatest Architects of the Twentieth Century*. New York: Abrams, 1994.

Picon, Antoine. *L'Art de l'ingénieur*. Paris: Centre Georges Pompidou, 1997.

Powell, Kenneth. *Grand Central Terminal, Warren and Wetmore*. London: Phaidon, 1996.

Richards, J. M. *An Introduction to Modern Architecture*. 3d ed. Harmondsworth, England: Penguin Books, 1962.

Rogers, E. N., J. L. Sert, and J. Tyrwhitt. *The Heart of the City: Towards the Humanisation of Urban Life*. International Congresses for Modern Architecture. New York: Pellegrini and Cudahy, 1952.

Rorty, Richard. "Introduction: Pragmatism and Philosophy." In *Consequences of Pragmatism*. Minneapolis: University of Minnesota Press, 1982.

Rowe, Colin. "The Present Urban Predicament." In *As I Was Saying, Recollections and Miscellaneous Essays*. Vol. 3. Cambridge, MA: MIT Press, 1996.

———, and Fred Koetter. *Collage City*. Cambridge, MA: MIT Press, 1978.

Rubino, Luciano. *Ray & Charles Eames, il colletivo della fantasia*. Rome: Kappa, 1981.

Rybczynski, Witold. *Home*. New York: Penguin, 1986.

Saarinen, Aline, ed. *Eero Saarinen on His Work*. New Haven: Yale University Press, 1962.

Saarinen, Eliel. *The City: Its Growth, Its Decay, Its Future*. New York: Reinhold Publishing Corporation, 1943.

Salvadori, Mario. *Why Buildings Stand Up: The Strength of Architecture*. New York: Norton, 1980.

Sartre, Jean-Paul. *L'existentialisme est un humanisme*. Paris: Nagel, 1946. Reprint. Paris: Gallimard, 1996

Schlesinger, Arthur M., Jr. *The Cycles of American History*. Boston: Houghton Mifflin, 1986.

Scott, Geoffrey. *The Architecture of Humanism: A Study in the History of Taste*. London: Constable, 1914. Reprint. Gloucester, MA: Peter Smith, 1965.

Scott, Mel. *American City Planning Since 1890*. Berkeley: University of California Press, 1969.

Scully, Vincent. *American Architecture and Urbanism*. New York: Henry Holt and Co., 1988.

Shapiro, Meyer. "Style." In Kroeber, A. L., ed. *Anthropology Today*. Chicago: University of Chicago Press, 1953.

Smithson, Alison, ed. *Team 10 Primer*. Cambridge, MA: MIT Press, 1974.

Spade, Rupert. Photographs by Yukio Futagawa. *Eero Saarinen*. Tokyo: Bijutsu Shuppan-sha, 1968. Reprint. New York: Simon and Schuster, 1971.

Stern, Robert A. M. *New Directions in American Architecture*. 2d ed. New York: George Braziller, 1977.

———, Thomas Mellins, and David Fishman. *New York 1960*. New York: Monacelli Press, 1995.

Tatarkiewicz, Wladyslaw. *A History of Six Ideas: An Essay in Aesthetics*. The Hague; Boston: Nijhoff; Hingham, MA., 1980.

Temko, Allan. *Eero Saarinen*. New York: George Braziller, 1962.

Thoreau, Henry David. "Civil Disobedience." In *Walden and Civil Disobedience*. Boston: 1849. Reprint. New York: Penguin Books, 1983.

Venturi, Robert. *Complexity and Contradiction in Architecture*. 2d ed. New York: Museum of Modern Art, 1977.

Virilio, Paul. *La vitesse de libération*. Paris: Galilée, 1995.

Weisman, Winston. "A New View of Skyscraper History." In Hitchcock, Henry-Russell, et al. *The Rise of an American Architecture*. London: Pall Mall Press; New York: Metropolitan Museum of Art, 1970.

Willis, Carol. *Form Follows Finance: Skyscrapers and Skylines in New York and Chicago*. New York: Princeton Architectural Press, 1995.

Woodward, Geo. E. *Woodward's Country Homes*. New York: Orange Judd and Co., 1865.

Wright, Frank Lloyd. *The Living City*. New York: Horizon Press, 1958.

Zevi, Bruno. *Storia dell'architettura moderna*. Torino: Giulio Einaudi, 1975.

PERIODICALS

"Architecture to Represent America Abroad." *Architectural Record* (May 1955): 187–92.

Arup, Ove. "Sydney Opera House." *Architectural Design* (March 1965): 134–42.

Atkinson, Fello. "U.S. Building, Grosvenor Square, London." *Architectural Review* (April 1961): 252–62.

Banham, Reyner. "The Obsolescent Airport." *Architectural Review* (October 1962): 252–53.

"Building Engineering." *Architectural Forum* (June 1953): 168–73.

Candela, Félix. "El escándalo de la Ópera de Sidney." *Arquitectura* (December 1967): 57–64.

Carter, Peter. "Eero Saarinen, 1910–1961." *Architectural Design* (December 1961): 537.

———. "Eero Saarinen as Furniture Designer." *Interior Design* (October 1957): 393.

"Competition, Jefferson National Expansion Memorial." *Progressive Architecture* (May 1948): 51–71.

"Concurso para la Ópera de Sidney." *Revista Nacional de Arquitectura* 187 (July 1957): 15–20.

"The Concrete Bird Stands Free." *Architectural Forum* (December 1960): 114–15.

"Controversial Building in London." *Architectural Forum* (March 1961): 80–85.

Dean, Andrea O. "Eero Saarinen in Perspective." *AIA Journal* (November 1981): 36–51.

"Distinguished Interior Architecture for CBS." *Architectural Record* (June 1966): 129–34.

Dorfles, Gillo. "Eero Saarinen: Recent Work." *Zodiac* 8, "America," 85–89.

"Dulles Airport Expansion." *Architecture* (November 1993): 40–41.

Fisher, Thomas. "Landmarks: TWA Terminal." *Progressive Architecture* (May 1992): 96–101.

"Four Great Pours" [Morandi, Candela, Saarinen, Nervi]. *Architectural Forum* (September 1961): 104–15.

"General Motors Technical Center." *Architectural Forum* (November 1951): 111–23.

"GM's Industrial Versailles." *Architectural Forum* (May 1956): 122–30.

"GM Nears Completion." *Architectural Forum* (November 1954).

"GM Technical Center." *Architectural Forum* (July 1949): 70–78.

Giedion, Sigfried. "Jørn Utzon and the Third Generation: A New Chapter of *Space, Time and Architecture*." *Zodiac 14* (1965): 36–47.

Guilford, J. P. "Creativity." *The American Psychologist* (September 1950): 444–54.

Haskell, Douglas. "Eero Saarinen, 1910–1961." *Architectural Forum* (October 1961): 96–97.

Hitchcock, Henry-Russell. "American Architecture in the Early Sixties."

Zodiac 10 (1962): 4–17.

"Idlewild, New York International Airport." *Architectural Record* (September 1961): 162–64.

"Jefferson National Expansion Memorial Competition." *Architectural Forum* (March 1948): 14–18.

Jencks, Charles. "Adhocism." *Architectural Review* (July 1968): 27–30.

Kidder Smith, G. E. "Report from Spain and Portugal." *Architectural Forum* (May 1950): 72 ff. See also "Concrete Stadium Canopies Shelter the Madrid Hippodrome," 130–31.

Knight, Carleton. "Whither Dulles? Cold War 'Landmark.'" *Progressive Architecture* (March 1978): 28.

Lebovich, William. "Redoing Dulles: Three Proposals." *Progressive Architecture* (April 1984): 28–29.

Lefaivre, Liane, and Alexander Tzonis. "The Machine in Architectural Thinking." *Daidalos* 18 (December 1985): 16–26.

Lessing, Lawrence. "The Diversity of Eero Saarinen." *Architectural Forum* (July 1960): 94–103.

Leubkeman, Christopher Hart. "Form Swallows Function." *Progressive Architecture* (May 1992): 106–9.

Lifchez, Raymond. "Eero Saarinen." *Zodiac* 17 (1967): 120–21.

MacKinnon, Donald W. "The Nature and Nurture of Creative Talent." *The American Psychologist* (July 1962): 484–95. Also published as "Nature et culture du talent créatif: hérédité et milieu" in Beaudot, Alain. *La créativité.* Paris: Bordas, 1973, 117–35.

McCue, George. "The Arch: An Appreciation." *AIA Journal* 67 (November 1978): 57–63.

McQuade, Walter. "Eero Saarinen: A Complete Architect." *Architectural Forum* (April 1962): 103–19.

Mies van der Rohe, Ludwig. "Bauen-Bauen." *G* 2 (September 1923).

Moneo, Rafael. "On Typology." *Oppositions* 13 (1978): 22–45.

———. "Sobre el escándalo de Sidney." *Arquitectura* (January 1968): 52–54.

"Music Tent." *Architectural Forum* (September 1949): 88–89.

"Music Tent." *Architectural Forum* (December 1958): 106–11.

Nakamura, Toshio, ed. "Eero Saarinen." *A+U* (April 1984).

"A New Airport for Jets." *Architectural Record* (March 1960): 175–82. On Dulles.

"A New Personality: Jørn Utzon." *Zodiac* 5 (1959): 70–105.

"New York Rethinks Its City Plan." *Architectural Forum* (September 1950): 122–27.

Papademetriou, Peter. "Coming of Age: Eero Saarinen and Modern American Architecture." *Perspecta* 21: 116–43.

———. "TWA's Influence." *Progressive Architecture* (May 1992): 102–5.

"Parabolic Cable Roof." *Architectural Forum* (June 1953): 168 ff.

"Passenger Terminal Buildings Design Principles." *Architectural Record* (March 1960): 167–82.

"'Polygonal' Architecture." *Architectural Record* (February 1960): 159–64.

"Pure Design Research." *Architectural Forum* (September 1952): 142–47. Work and statements by Harry Bertoia.

Rowe, Colin, and Fred Koetter. "The Crisis of the Object: The Predicament of Texture." *Perspecta* 16 (1980): 109–42.

Saarinen, Eero. "Campus Planning: The Unique World of the University." *Architectural Record* (November 1960): 123–30.

———. "The Changing Philosophy of Architecture." *Architectural Record* (August 1954): 182.

———. "Recent Work of Eero Saarinen." *Zodiac* 4: 30–67.

———. "The Six Broad Currents of Modern Architecture." *Architectural Forum* (July 1953): 110–15.

Saarinen, Susan. "Susan Saarinen's Interview in Helsinki, June 23, 1995." Interview by Aino Niskanen and Timo Tuomi. *Ptah* 1 (1998): 26–31.

"Saarinen." *Architectural Forum* (September 1961): 112–13. On Dulles.

"Saarinen's CBS Design." *Architectural Record* (April 1962): 149–50.

"Saarinen's Skyscraper." *Architectural Record* (July 1965): 111–18.

"Shaping a Two-Acre Sculpture." *Architectural Forum* (August 1960): 118–23.

Solà-Morales, Ignasi. "Arquitectura débil." *Quaderns* 175 (1987): 72–85.

———. "Architettura e esistenzialismo: una crisi dell'architettura moderna" *Casabella* 583 (October 1991): 38–40. Published as "Arquitectura y existencialismo" in *Diferencias. Topografía de la arquitectura contemporánea.* Barcelona: Gustavo Gili, 1995.

"SOM's Addition to Dulles International Airport Respects Eero Saarinen's 'Modern Masterpiece.'" *Architectural Record* (March 1997): 62–67.

"TWA's Graceful Air Terminal." *Architectural Forum* (January 1958): 78–85.

"U.S. Architecture Abroad." *Architectural Forum* (March 1953): 101–15.

"Utzon: The Sidney Opera House." *Nueva Forma* (January-February 1974).

Utzon, Jørn. "Platforms and Plateaus: Ideas of a Danish Architect." *Zodiac* 10 (1962): 112–40.

Wright, Frank Lloyd. "In the Cause of Architecture II." *Architectural Record* (May 1914). Also published in Gutheim, Frederick, ed. *Frank Lloyd Wright on Architecture: Selected Writings, 1894–1940.* New York: Duell, Sloan and Pearce, 1941.

"Yale's Viking Vessel." *Architectural Forum* (December 1958): 106–11.

Zevi, Bruno. "Pluralismo e pop-architectura." *L'Architettura* (September 1967): 282–83.

Work in collaboration with Eliel Saarinen, 1936–50
First Christian Church, Columbus, Indiana, 1939
Crow Island School, Winnetka, Illinois, 1939
Antioch College, Yellow Springs, Ohio: campus plan, 1946; dormitory, 1947
Brandeis University, Waltham, Massachusetts: campus plan, 1948;
    dormitory, dining, and social buildings, 1949–50
Berkshire Music Center, Lenox, Massachusetts: Tanglewood Shed, 1940
Christ Church Lutheran, Minneapolis, Minnesota, 1949
Smithsonian Art Gallery Competition, Washington, DC, first prize, 1939

Independent work, 1941–64
Community House project, 1941
Unfolding House project, 1945
Music Tent, Aspen, Colorado, 1949
Jefferson National Expansion Memorial, St. Louis, Missouri, 1948–64
General Motors Technical Center, Warren, Michigan
    (with Smith, Hinchman & Grylls, architects-engineers), 1948–56
Drake University, Des Moines, Iowa: Pharmacy Building, 1947–50;
    dormitories and dining hall, 1951–55
Irwin Union Trust Company, Columbus, Indiana, 1952–55
Massachusetts Institute of Technology, Cambridge, Massachusetts:
    auditorium and chapel, 1953–56
Master plan, University of Michigan, Ann Arbor, Michigan, 1954
Milwaukee County War Memorial, Milwaukee, Wisconsin, 1953–57
Stephens College Chapel, Columbia, Missouri, 1953–57
Miller House, Columbus, Indiana, 1953–57
Concordia Senior College, Fort Wayne, Indiana, 1953–58
Vassar College, Poughkeepsie, New York: dormitory, 1954–58
University of Chicago, Illinois: women's dormitory and dining hall, 1955–58
U.S. Embassy, Oslo, Norway, 1955–59
U.S. Embassy, London, England, 1955–60
University of Chicago, Illinois: law school, 1956–62
International Business Machines, Rochester, Minnesota, 1956–59
David S. Ingalls Hockey Rink, Yale University, New Haven, Connecticut, 1956–59
TWA Terminal, Queens, New York, 1956–62
University of Pennsylvania, Philadelphia, Pennsylvania: women's dormitories, 1957–60
Deere & Company, Moline, Illinois, 1957–63
IBM Thomas J. Watson Research Center, Yorktown, New York, 1957–61
Bell Laboratories, Holmdel, New Jersey, 1957–62
Ezra Stiles and Morse colleges, Yale University, New Haven, Connecticut, 1958–62
Dulles International Airport Terminal Building, Chantilly, Virginia
    (with Ammann & Whitney, architects-engineers), 1958–62
Repertory Theater and Library Museum, Lincoln Center for the Performing Arts, New York, New York
    (with Skidmore, Owings & Merrill and Jo Mielziner, collaborating designer for Repertory Theatre),
    1958–64
International Airport, Athens, Greece (with Ammann & Whitney, architects-engineers), 1960–64
North Christian Church, Columbus, Indiana, 1959–63
CBS Building, New York, New York, 1960–64

Furniture design
Organic Design Furniture, Museum of Modern Art Competition (with Charles Eames), 1938
Plywood Chair (for Knoll Associates), 1946
Womb Chair (for Knoll Associates), 1948
Pedestal furniture (for Knoll Associates), 1958
Assorted furniture, General Motors Technical Center, 1950

ACKNOWLEDGMENTS

I am grateful to all those whose generous contributions have made this study possible. First I thank architect Kevin Roche for the warm welcome he gave me at his office in Hamden, Connecticut. The conversations we held there were an essential help and an invaluable source of inspiration. Mr. Roche and his staff put at my disposal all the resources of his office, and allowed me to do crucial research in the Eero Saarinen Archive. I also thank architect Cesar Pelli for receiving me so enthusiastically at his office in New Haven, Connecticut, and for his invaluable and always passionate thoughts on Eero Saarinen.

Peter Papademetriou was an exceptional guide to the Eero Saarinen Archive; his thorough knowledge of the documents was a great help. In turn, Judith Ann Schiff, Yale Manuscripts and Archives Chief Research Archivist, and her staff put at my disposal the Eero Saarinen Papers along with other pertinent documents in the Yale collection. Mark Coir, the Cranbrook Archives and Cultural Properties Director, Cranbrook Educational Community, and his staff allowed me to consult the Cranbrook collections, notably the Saarinen Family Papers. Such was their hospitality and enthusiasm that Eero Saarinen seemed to be ever-present during my stay in Bloomfield Hills, Michigan. Lisa Hodermarsky, in charge of Yale Art Gallery Archives, kindly provided me with access to the watercolors and drawings of the Saarinen Collection. The invariably incisive comments of architectural critic and historian Philip Drew were crucial to my understanding of the Sydney Opera House competition. I thank Stanton Wheeler, Kenneth Cooper, Mary Woodbeck, and Lynwood Dent who made possible my visits to the Yale colleges, the CBS Building, the General Motors Technical Center, and the American Embassy in London, respectively. In addition, I am greatly indebted to the personnel of the several libraries I worked at during this project, particularly those in Spain, such as the schools of architecture of the Universidad Politécnica de Madrid and Universitat Politècnica de Catalunya, Architectural Societies in Madrid, Barcelona, and Bilbao, and the Universidad de Deusto, Bilbao. Rodolfo Machado has been steadfast in his support since I studied with him at Harvard University. I am also indebted to all those who offered me academic or professional support during different stages of the research process, including Rafael Moneo, Jorge Silvetti, Daniel Schodek, Gabriel Ruiz Cabrero, Javier Cenicacelaya, Juan Antonio Cortés, Marta Llorente, José Manuel López-Peláez, Pedro Moleón, Miguel Ángel Alonso, José Barbeito, Iñaki Ábalos, Josep Maria Montaner, and José María González Pinto. I am also grateful to Mark Hounsell, who, with his insightful editorial comments, oversaw the translation from the Spanish manuscript. Princeton Architectural Press has spared no effort in editing and publishing the book, which received the inestimable support of the Graham Foundation for Advanced Studies in the Fine Arts.

It would not have been possible to complete my doctoral dissertation, the basis for the this text, without the counsel of José Ignacio Linazasoro and the supervision of my principal advisor, Ignasi de Solà-Morales. With great enthusiasm and commitment, he encouraged me to turn that study into this book. Finally, I thank my parents, who have always inspired me in my endeavor to explore the enigma of Eero Saarinen.

INDEX